D1314531

THE
RHYTHM
OF JEWISH
TIME

THE RHYTHM OF JEWISH TIME

An
Introduction
to Holidays
and Life-Cycle
Events

Edited by Vicki L. Weber

BEHRMAN HOUSE, INC.

2964
w

Project Editor: Vicki L. Weber
Book Design: Pronto Design and Production, Inc.
Artwork: Joni Liberman, Erika Weihs
Cover Design: Pronto Design and Production, Inc.
Cover: details from "The Four Seasons,"
A mosaic created for and given to the people of Chicago
By Marc Chagall.
Owned by Art in the Center/Sited and
maintained by The First National Bank of Chicago

The editor and publisher gratefully acknowledge the cooperation of the following sources of photographs for this book:

Israel Museum/David Harris, 13; **Sotheby's, Inc.**, 18, 24, 68; **UAHC**, 22; **Peter Wallburg Studio**, 27; **Beth Hatefutsoth, Photo Archive, Tel Aviv**, 32, 113; **Bill Aron**, 36, 57, 63, 103, 134, 141; **April Saul**, 39, 155; **Jewish Museum** 42, 44, 46, 50, 51, 64, 65, 73, 106, 111, 115, 119, 125, 135, 136, 137, 138; **Amy Saul-Zerby**, 53; **E. Brandon**, 59; **Creative Image Photography**, 67, 91, 97, 126, 138, 143, 145; **New York Public Library**, 69; **Alan Carey/The Image Works**, 75; **State Museum in Prague**, 79, 80, 82, 83, 88; **Edinburgh University Library**, 100; **Jewish Community Center of Cleveland**, 102; **HUC Museum**, 105; **Israel Office of Information**, 109, 117; **L. Goldman/R. Guillumette**, 123; **Francine Keery**, 124, 136, 143, 145, 149, 156, 159, 161.

Library of Congress Cataloging-in-Publication Data:
Weber, Vicki L.
    The rhythm of Jewish time: an introduction to holidays and lifecycle events.
        p.   cm.
    Edited by Vicki L. Weber
    Includes index.
    ISBN 0-87441-673-6
    1. Judaism--Customs and practices. 2. Life cycle, Human--Religious aspects--Judaism.
3. Fasts and feasts--Judaism. 4. Jewish Families--Religious life.
    I. Title.
    BM700.W34   1999
    296.4--dc21   98-34736

                                                                                   CIP

Copyright © 1999 by Behrman House, Inc.
235 Watchung Avenue, West Orange, New Jersey 07052
All rights reserved
ISBN 0-87441-673-6
Printed in the United States of America

Contents

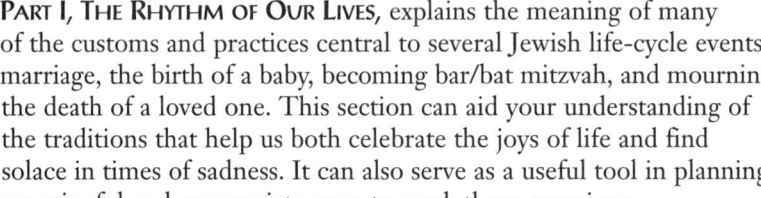

How to Use This Book

The Rhythm of Time: An Introduction to Jewish Holidays and Life-Cycle Events is primarily a "how to" book, to help you bring Jewish traditions into your life and home by taking you, step by step, through the rituals, blessings, and special customs of the family events and holidays that mark our lives as Jews. You may find you want to read it through all at once, or you might prefer to seek out the specific events, holidays, or blessings you are most interested in right now.

PART I, THE RHYTHM OF OUR LIVES, explains the meaning of many of the customs and practices central to several Jewish life-cycle events: marriage, the birth of a baby, becoming bar/bat mitzvah, and mourning the death of a loved one. This section can aid your understanding of the traditions that help us both celebrate the joys of life and find solace in times of sadness. It can also serve as a useful tool in planning meaningful and appropriate ways to mark these occasions.

PART II, THE RHYTHM OF OUR YEAR, is designed to help you bring the holidays alive for your own family. Shared holiday experiences can draw you and your family together in a unique closeness. This section presents a brief sketch of each of the holidays, describing a little of its history and the ways it is celebrated both at home and in the synagogue. Suggestions for involving children in the celebration of each holiday are also included. A special chapter on Shabbat leads you through your own Friday night home celebration and provides background on the nature and meaning of our weekly holiday.

   **PART III, THE RHYTHM OF OUR HOMES,** is a reference to help you choose rituals to perform as you celebrate the holidays. Judaism is primarily a home-focused way of life. In this section you will find a guide to the basic ritual objects that will help you bring Judaism into your home. Part III also contains the blessings and prayers usually included in the home service for each holiday. The text of the blessings is provided in both English and Hebrew, along with a transliteration. Finally, because the flavor of so many holidays comes from special foods we eat, some popular holiday recipes are provided, along with a brief guide to *kashrut*, the traditional dietary laws of Judaism.

You don't have to know everything about Jewish life-cycle events and festivals to bring them into your family's life. Sometimes how you *feel* about an occasion is more important than how much you *know*. When you need answers to your own or your family's questions, turn to this handbook for guidance. Beyond that, you can always ask your rabbi or a Jewish educator.

If you have not been celebrating life-cycle events or the holidays in a Jewish way, we hope this book will encourage you to begin. If you have already established some home rituals for Shabbat and the holidays, we hope you will find some ideas here to increase your enjoyment of these special times and to help you build a cycle of home celebrations that truly belongs to you and your family.

The Rhythm of Our Lives:

A Guide to Jewish Life-Cycle Events

ON GETTING MARRIED

ON THE BIRTH OF A BABY

ON BECOMING BAR/BAT MITZVAH

ON THE DEATH OF A LOVED ONE

On Getting Married

"God creates new worlds constantly

by causing marriages to take place."

ZOHAR 1:89a

Mazal Tov!

The phone rings. An excited voice announces, "Rabbi, great news! We're engaged to be married, and we want you to perform the wedding ceremony."

Such calls are always filled with joy and the anticipation of an event that will be one of the most important in every couple's life, just as it is in yours. Emotions run high as you chart the course of a new life together.

One of the first subjects to command attention, of course, is the planning of the wedding itself—the ceremony that will solemnize your feelings for one another, and the festivities that will celebrate your union.

You will soon discover that your marriage is not only the union of two individuals, but indeed the joining of two families. This is a good time to set a pattern of compromise, for the wedding day will pass but your life together will span the decades. Don't allow minor details to provide the basis for future discord. Rather, let your wedding day be just the first of many joyous occasions celebrated together by your two newly joined families. Let it be the cornerstone of a long and happy life based on trust, love, and companionship.

The specific choices you will make concerning your wedding day are many. I would like to outline some of the issues frequently faced by engaged couples, in the hope that they will help you make your plans as well as stimulate discussions between the two of you. Perhaps they will also lead you to additional questions which your own rabbi can answer.

The choices you make will shape your wedding day into a truly memorable and personal experience. The unique customs and traditions of our Jewish heritage can make it a spiritual and beautiful experience for all who share it with you.

I hope that this chapter will help you make knowledgeable choices as you plan the details of your wedding day.

Congratulations! Mazal Tov!
Ron Isaacs

Planning Your Wedding

Jewish Tradition and the Engaged Couple

The importance of marriage in the Jewish tradition is summed up in the talmudic statement that when one marries, one becomes a complete person. Marriage is regarded as the ideal state. In the very first book of the Bible, God tells Adam that it is not good for man to live alone.

Marriage is considered a *mitzvah*, a divine commandment. When a Jewish couple marries, it becomes possible for them to fulfill Judaism's first biblical obligation: "be fruitful and multiply." A Jewish marriage celebrates the creation of a new Jewish family. With the arrival of its first child, that family becomes God's partner

A Jewish wedding.

Oil on canvas by Mouryey Gottlieb (1856–1879).

in the ongoing process of creation. For this reason text in the *Zohar* (an early work of the Kabbalah) says, "God is constantly creating new worlds by causing marriages to take place."

It is interesting to note that there is no single, precise word for marriage in Hebrew. The Bible speaks only of "taking a wife." Many years ago our sages used the word *kiddushin* (sanctification) to mean marriage. This expression reflects the spirituality and holiness that are an integral part of the husband–wife relationship.

In Jewish literature God is often portrayed as a *shadkhan*, a matchmaker.

A rabbinic parable describes a confrontation between a skeptical Roman matron and Rabbi Yose ben Chalafta. The woman asked the rabbi, "In how many days did God create the world?"

"In six days," the rabbi answered.

"What has your God been doing since then?" she asked.

The rabbi replied, "God makes marriages, assigning this man to that woman, and this woman to that man."

The story goes on to tell how the matron, unimpressed, quickly married off all her household slaves, two by two, claiming that she could do the same as Rabbi Yose's God. The very next day the villa resounded with complaints and protests from the newly married couples. Finally the matron relented. She summoned Rabbi Yose and admitted, "There is no God like your God."

Judaism has always viewed marriage as a sacred agreement between two loving companions. This exalted partnership has even been compared to the covenantal bond which God established with the Jewish people when they were chosen to be God's treasured nation.

Of all the happy occasions in the Jewish life cycle, the wedding is the celebration of celebrations—the *simḥah* of *simḥahs*. The consecration of a marriage is such cause for rejoicing that no other festivity is allowed to interfere with it. Throughout the ages the wedding ceremony was an occasion to be shared by the entire Jewish community, and it was the community's responsibility to do everything possible to ensure the happiness of every bride and groom. Since antiquity the celebration of a marriage has included music, feasting, dancing, and jesting. In fact, in many communities of old the festivities continued for an entire week! Even today many traditional couples celebrate each evening of the first week of their marriage in the company of friends and family.

"My soul takes pleasure in three things

for they are beautiful to Adonai and to all people:

harmony within families, friendship among neighbors,

and a husband and wife suited to each other."

BEN SIRA 25:1

Your wedding day will likely be the quintessential event in your life. It is a consecration, a sanctification of life itself. The Ba'al Shem Tov, founder of Ḥasidism, said it well: "From every human being there rises a light that reaches to heaven. When two souls are destined to find each other, their streams of light flow together, and a single brighter light goes forth from their united being."

Selecting a Date and Place for the Wedding

As you begin to plan for your wedding day, you will soon find that every decision seems to depend upon another. The first thing to do is to choose a date. Once you establish the exact date and time for your wedding, other decisions will be easier to make.

How you choose your wedding date will, to some extent, reflect your personal priorities. If it is important for you to have a particular rabbi or cantor officiate at the wedding, you will have to take into account their schedules and prior commitments. Similarly, you may want to consider the availability of your close family and special friends. In addition, it is important to consider your own work and vacation schedules. The season of the year, climate, and weather are other factors you might consider.

Jewish tradition also places some limitations on the choice of a wedding date. For instance, weddings are never held on the Sabbath or on festivals so that we do not mix—and consequently dilute—each joyous occasion. In addition, marriage is considered a legal transaction, and business transactions are not permitted on the Sabbath and festivals. Days that commemorate tragic events in Jewish history are also not appropriate times for a marriage celebration (*Sefirah* period, between Passover and Shavuot, the Three Weeks leading to Tishah b'Av, minor fast days). There is some variation in the observance of these special days, so be sure to consult with your rabbi before making the final selection of your wedding date.

There are no Jewish laws restricting the selection of the location for your wedding and reception. There are, however, some guidelines to consider.

There is probably no finer way to highlight the spiritual nature of your wedding than to hold the ceremony in a synagogue sanctuary. This setting provides an aura of sanctity and spirituality. If you have a personal attachment to your synagogue, you will feel especially comfortable in the familiar surroundings which will call to mind other happy celebrations held there.

If you do decide to get married in a synagogue, the synagogue's social hall is an attractive and convenient choice for the reception. However, hotels and catering establishments are certainly viable alternatives.

Outdoor weddings, too, are not only acceptable but indeed rooted in Jewish tradition. Customarily, outdoor weddings, especially those held in the evening, were considered to bring good luck because the bride and groom could see the stars, which would remind them of God's promise to Abraham that the Jewish people would be as prolific as the stars in the sky.

Weddings held in the home of the bride or groom have always been in fashion. A home can add an atmosphere of warmth and intimacy and is ideal if you want an informal ceremony in an intimate setting.

No matter which location you choose, it is important to consider your own as well as your guests' comfort and travel arrangements. If any of the guests are elderly or handicapped, you should check into the accessibility of the location (e.g., ramps and/or elevators).

Your choice of where to be married might well be influenced by the kind of cuisine available at a particular place. Because the Jewish wedding is considered a religious as well as a social occasion, the meal served is an integral part of the ritual, a *seudat mitzvah* (ritually prescribed feast). It is therefore altogether proper and fitting for the wedding feast to be a kosher meal. You will be happy to find that the inclusion of a kosher meal in your wedding festivities will add an extra measure of spirituality and Jewish flavor to your very important day.

Who Will Officiate?

An ordained rabbi or cantor may perform a wedding that is recognized both Jewishly and civilly. If your family is affiliated with a synagogue, your own rabbi is the best choice. A rabbi who knows you and your family will add a personal touch of warmth to the ceremony.

If your family is unaffiliated, seek out people whose opinion you trust to help you find appropriate clergy. If you are a student, the campus Hillel rabbi might be the logical choice.

You may, of course, have more than one officiant. It is not unusual to have both the bride and the groom represented by each family's rabbi and/or cantor. It is accepted protocol for the host rabbi to contact the visiting clergy prior to the wedding day so that they may plan the ceremony together.

You should arrange a meeting with the rabbi well before your wedding day. Come prepared with questions to discuss. Here are some points you might like to discuss with the rabbi:

- The format of the ceremony, and how much Hebrew will be incorporated into it.
- The inclusion of personal elements in the ceremony (poems, readings, your own vows).
- The honorarium or charitable contribution for the services of the clergy.
- The kind of *ketubah* (marriage contract) the rabbi uses.

Come prepared with your Hebrew names and those of your parents. The rabbi will need this information to complete the *ketubah*.

The rabbi will be able to tell you where to apply for the civil marriage license and when and where to take the required blood tests.

Increasingly, couples are deciding to be tested for Tay Sachs disease and other genetic disorders to which some Jewish populations seem statistically susceptible. You might want to discuss this matter with the rabbi as well.

Choosing Wedding Apparel, Rings, and Music

Our religious laws do not stipulate what a bride or groom must wear. However, interesting customs have developed over the years.

The Talmud often compares a bride and groom to a king and queen. In those times the bride and groom were often seated on throne-like chairs, wearing crowns and wreaths as part of their regal costume.

Jews in each country have developed their own particular style of wedding dress. In some countries the dress is very ornate. Jewish brides in Iraq, for example, wear silver bells and golden nose rings. In Arab countries Jewish brides wear necklaces and headdresses of gold and silver.

Elaborate gold marriage ring with miniature building at the top carrying the Hebrew inscription *Mazal tov* (good luck).

The most common custom among Jews with an Eastern European tradition, as among the general American population, is for a bride to wear white, a symbol of purity. The bride wears a veil at the ceremony, reminiscent of the biblical Rebeccah, who covered her face when she first saw her future husband, Isaac.

For the groom, the traditional custom is to wear over his wedding suit, a *kittel*, a simple white robe, which denotes purity, humility, and festivity.

In selecting your own wedding attire, keep in mind that Judaism frowns upon needless extravagance. Modesty is very much in keeping with our tradition.

The giving and accepting of an item of value in the presence of witnesses is the most important part of the Jewish wedding ceremony. In earlier times, coins were used as the preferred object of exchange. Each country had its own custom as to how a bride was to accept the gift. For example, brides in Baghdad wore silk gloves to demonstrate that their acceptance of the coin was not to be construed as charity.

It has become almost universal Jewish practice, with the exception of only a few Oriental communities, to use a ring as the token of the marriage bond. Just as a ring has no beginning and no end, so too it is the wish of every bride and groom that their love be complete and unending.

Jewish law states that every ring must meet three standards:

- It must belong to the groom.
- It must be of solid metal, customarily gold.
- It cannot have gems or stones in it.

One ring, given by the groom to his bride, is required. However, double-ring ceremonies, in which both bride and groom exchange rings, can usually take place in Reform and Conservative weddings. While the gift of coins or a ring was originally conceived as a token of acquisition, in a contemporary setting, the double exchange of rings expresses a partnership, with a mutuality of respect and an equality of status. Be sure to consult with your rabbi before purchasing your ring(s).

....

"God has dressed me with garments

of exultation. . . As a bridegroom puts

on a priestly diadem and a bride

adorns herself with jewels."

....

ISAIAH 61:10

Music, with its power to elicit strong expressions of joy and tender expressions of love, has always been an integral part of the Jewish wedding ceremony and celebration. Even in biblical times, marriage processions were often accompanied by musicians. And later, in talmudic times, some rabbis would lead the wedding guests in responsive singing.

In choosing the music for your wedding ceremony, you have an opportunity to fashion a unique and meaningful setting. There are many Jewish folk, liturgical, and even modern melodies from which to choose. If you do not have the knowledge to make educated choices, be sure to consult with the cantor of your synagogue. The traditional American "Here Comes the Bride" is usually avoided, since it was composed by Wagner, a known anti-Semite. By selecting music that echoes our Jewish heritage, you can transform your ceremonial march down the aisle into a beautiful and moving experience.

The music at the party following the ceremony can range from the single voice of one acoustical or electronic instrument to the collective sound of a small band or a large orchestra. The size of the room and the number of guests are important factors to consider. Decide on the kind of mood you would like to create. If you plan a quiet, intimate party where conversation among your guests is of primary concern, a single musician or a few strolling violinists might be your choice. If, on the other hand, you want an upbeat affair with dancing as the main focus, a band with a strong rhythm section might suit you better.

The inclusion of Israeli and traditional Jewish wedding dances always adds a large measure of *freilichkeit* (joyousness) to a wedding celebration. When you interview musicians, be sure to ask if this music is in their repertoire. If the director is not familiar with any particular selection you want played, you may provide a recording or sheet music a few weeks in advance.

The Ketubah *and the* Ḥuppah

The *ketubah* is a Jewish legal document which confirms the religious bonds of your union. It does not take the place of a standard civil marriage license, which the rabbi will need in order to perform the ceremony.

The *ketubah*, in one form or another, has been used by Jews for more than two thousand years. The traditional *ketubah* is written in Aramaic, the language of the Jews exiled in Babylonia. The earliest formulation of the *ketubah* is found in the Talmud and was written by Shimon ben Shetach, president of the ancient rabbinic court. Two thousand years later we still use his words. The great innovation of the Jewish marriage

Elaborate *ketubot* were used in Italy beginning in the sixteenth century. They were often decorated with compositions of fruits, flowers, and birds. Illuminated parchment marriage contract.
livorno, Italy 1748

document is its recognition that not only love but also legal commitment is necessary in a Jewish marriage.

The husband's primary obligations are listed in the *ketubah*. He must cherish and honor his wife and provide for her support and sexual fulfillment. His financial obligations in case of divorce are also spelled out to ensure the woman sufficient funds should the marriage be terminated. Many new *ketubot* include two parallel declarations of commitment by both bride and groom.

The *ketubah* can be a beautiful work of art. Should you decide to join the growing number of couples who have a *ketubah* designed especially for them, be sure to commission an artist well in advance so that it will be ready in time for your wedding day. The artist must also confer with your rabbi as to the exact wording and variable spellings of Hebrew names and places.

Two witnesses are required for the signing of the *ketubah*. They sign it in Hebrew. Jewish law requires that legal witnesses be adult, religiously observant, and not related by blood or marriage to either the bride or groom or to each other. The officiating rabbi and cantor can serve as witnesses unless they are related to the bride or groom. Orthodox rabbis will allow only males to serve as witnesses. Reform and some Conservative rabbis will permit women to participate. Since your witnesses will be asked to sign their complete names in Hebrew, remind them to prepare for this requirement. Serving as a witness to a Jewish marriage is an honor and an important responsibility. Do choose your witnesses carefully. A *ḥuppah* is the wedding canopy under which the bride and groom stand during the marriage ceremony. (It is optional at Reform weddings.) The *ḥuppah* symbolizes the home that the bride and groom will create as husband and wife.

The wedding canopy has an interesting history. In biblical times the meaning of the word *ḥuppah* was "room" or "covering." The Book of Joel states: "Let the bridegroom go forth from his chamber and the bride out of her pavilion (*ḥuppah*)."

During the rabbinic era the *ḥuppah* referred to the bridal chamber erected by the groom's father and covered with purple cloth, a sign of royalty. Centuries later, when outdoor weddings became very popular, the *ḥuppah* took the form of a portable fabric canopy rather than a fixed structure.

In ancient Israel it was customary to plant a tree on the occasion of the birth of a child. When the child married, the branches from that tree were used as poles and the leaves as decoration for the wedding canopy.

Among Sephardic Jews and some German Jews it is customary to drape a large prayer shawl, *tallit*, around the bride and groom.

Today wedding canopies are available in many sizes, colors, and styles. Some are made from fiber, others are floral. A *ḥuppah* can be as simple as a *tallit* held up by four poles, or quite elaborate. Be sure to inquire about the canopy that will be used at your ceremony. If you want it decorated with flowers or greenery, inform your florist. Some synagogues and reception halls have several *ḥuppah* styles from which to choose. Like the other choices you will be making, your selection of a particular style of *ḥuppah* can reflect your own tastes.

Special Traditions: Tenaim, Aufruf, *and* Mikveh

Years ago most Jewish marriages were arranged through a matchmaker, a *shadkhan*. This practice dates back to biblical times. In the Book of Genesis we read that

Abraham's servant was sent on a mission to find an appropriate bride for Isaac. His search was successful, and Rebeccah, who stood out because of her extreme kindness, became Isaac's bride and Judaism's second matriarch.

In talmudic times, as soon as a match was arranged, the parents of the bride and groom negotiated the terms of the dowry. These terms were set forth in a contract called *tenaim*, which means "stipulations." This contract was legally binding, and a fine or penalty was imposed if either party reneged on the arrangement. In European communities the *tenaim* were often officially sealed by the breaking of a dinner plate, an act that corresponds to the breaking of the glass at the wedding ceremony. Eastern communities developed other traditions surrounding the *tenaim*, often including the exchange of gifts.

" I will betroth you with righteousness, with

justice, with love, and compassion."

HOSEA 2:21

Today, although some still practice these customs, we are not required to set forth *tenaim*. Also, because arranged marriages are less common in our time, the ceremony has lost its popularity. It is interesting that some couples have reinterpreted the practice by formalizing a prenuptial contract relating to the couple's life together. It can include the desired number of children, finances, professional careers, the role of religion, and so forth.

The *aufruf* ceremony is a unique occasion to honor the groom and his bride. The word *aufruf* is derived from the German, meaning "calling up." It refers to the "calling up" of the groom-to-be, and sometimes the bride, to the Torah for an *aliyah*. The groom is called to the *bimah* just before the reading of the Torah portion for that day. In many Conservative and Reform congregations the bride shares her groom's *aliyah* or receives one of her own. It may also be customary to offer honors to the parents and grandparents of the bride and groom. The origin of the custom of *aufruf* is ascribed to King Solomon, who, it is told, had his attendants perform kindnesses for a groom on the Sabbath preceding his wedding day. Today the *aufruf* gives public recognition to a forthcoming marriage. We take joy and pride in welcoming the newest Jewish family-to-be to the community.

The *aufruf* is usually scheduled on the Sabbath immediately prior to the wedding. If that Sabbath is inconvenient, the *aufruf* can take place on an earlier Sabbath or during a weekday service when the Torah is read (Monday, Thursday, or Rosh Ḥodesh). The *aufruf* can be held in the synagogue of either the bride or the groom. If neither family is affiliated with a synagogue, arrangements can be made by contacting a local congregation.

Each person called to the Torah chants two blessings—one before the Torah reading and one after—but a person trained in Torah reading, called a *ba'al keriah* (masc.) or *ba'alat keriah* (fem.), does the actual reading from the Torah.

The first blessing, called the *Birkhot Ha-Torah*, praises God for choosing us from all nations and giving us Torah.

Barekhu et-Adonai ha-mevorakh.
Barukh Adonai ha-mevorakh le'olam va'ed.
Barukh atah, Adonai Eloheinu, melekh ha-olam,
asher baḥar-banu mikol-ha-amim,
ve'natan-lanu et-torato.
Barukh atah, Adonai, noten ha-Torah.

Praise Adonai, who is praised.
Praised is Adonai, who is praised forever and ever.
Praised are You, Adonai our God, Ruler of the world,
who chose us from all the nations,
and gave us the Torah.
Praised are You, Adonai, who gives us the Torah.

The blessing after the reading of the Torah praises God for giving us the truth of the Torah and for the eternal life Torah gives us.

Barukh atah, Adonai Eloheinu, melekh ha-olam,
asher natan-lanu torat emet veḥayei olam nata betokhenu.
Barukh atah, Adonai, noten ha-Torah.

Praised are You, Adonai our God, Ruler of the world,
who gave us the Torah of truth, and implanted within us eternal life.
Praised are You, Adonai, who gives us the Torah.

During the *aufruf* the rabbi may also recite a prayer on behalf of the couple.

Some congregations, following an old custom, throw nuts, raisins, and candies after the *aliyah* or after the rabbi blesses the couple. These foods symbolize the wish for a sweet and fruitful, prosperous life. This is a lovely, fun-filled custom to follow. Be aware, however, that candies sweet to the tastebuds can be painful when thrown to other parts of the face. It is a good idea to choose very small candies and to wrap them so they may be eaten even if they land on the floor.

At the conclusion of the Sabbath services, it is customary for the family of the groom and bride to invite the congregation to a *kiddush*, Sabbath refreshments. In this way the *mitzvah* of hospitality is fulfilled and everyone present may share in the celebration.

With all the many demands made on you during this hectic time, it is natural to become caught up in the details of preparation and all too easy to forget the spiritual aspect of the momentous occasion that awaits you.

One way in which this spiritual need can be fulfilled is for the bride-to-be to go the *mikveh*, the ritual bath, on a night preceding the wedding. *Mikveh*, a Hebrew term meaning "gathering of water," refers to the public ritual bath that has for centuries been maintained by every Jewish community. The use of a *mikveh* is a requirement of traditional Jewish law for the purpose of purification and cleanliness of the body. A matron will be present to guide the bride-to-be through the brief ritual and to assist her. As a rule, *mikveh* attendants encourage a prospective bride

Eighteenth century engraving of the *mikveh* in Amsterdam.

to call for an appointment. In some Orthodox communities it is also customary for the groom to visit the *mikveh* on the morning of the wedding or on the Friday afternoon preceding it.

Celebrating Your Wedding

Before the Ceremony Begins

Before the start of the formal wedding ceremony, the *ketubah* is signed. In a symbolic act known as *kinyan*, the groom accepts a material object from the rabbi, usually a handkerchief, lifts it, and then returns it, thereby demonstrating his willingness to fulfill his obligations as stipulated in the *ketubah*. The two witnesses then sign their names to the document.

There are variations in the customs related to the signing of the *ketubah*. Some Conservative and Reform rabbis have both bride and groom sign, each in the presence of the same two witnesses. In some Reform weddings no provision is made for a *ketubah*, while in others a revised document is used.

Bedeken, or veiling ceremony, also takes place before the actual wedding ceremony. It is generally not a Reform custom. During the *bedeken*, the groom comes to officially "claim" his bride. The groom lowers the veil over his bride's face. According to one interpretation, this veiling ceremony developed to prevent a recurrence of what happened to Jacob in biblical times. Laban, Rachel's father, tricked the groom Jacob by substituting his older daughter, Leah, who wore an opaque veil. In order to avoid Jacob's dilemma, it has become customary for the groom to personally lower the veil over his bride's face. Others view the veiling of the bride as an act of modesty, as Rebeccah veiled herself when she first met Isaac, her betrothed.

"Grant perfect joy to these loving companions. . ."

SHEVA BRACHOT

After the bride is veiled, the groom or the bride's father recites the blessing given to Rebeccah by her mother and brother before she left her home to marry Isaac: "Our sister, be thou the mother of thousands, of ten thousands." This blessing is often followed by the Priestly Blessing: "May God Bless you and keep you. May God shine His countenance upon you and be gracious unto you. May God turn His presence toward you and favor you with peace."

The custom of escorting the bride and groom to the *huppah* is an ancient one. An early midrashic story attributes this practice to God, who was described as "bringing" Eve to Adam. Throughout Jewish history brides and grooms have been compared to kings and queens, who always appear with an entourage. The tradition of attendants continues to this day. It is a great joy for parents, grandparents, sisters, brothers, and close friends to lead the bride and groom to their wedding canopy.

The order of the procession and the number of participants is not fixed by Jewish law. However, some customs have continued over the years, and these may help serve as guides.

Since Judaism has always emphasized the important role of parents, the bride and groom most commonly are escorted by both their parents.

The role of the best man and maid or matron of honor has an early precedent. Legend has it that Michael and Gabriel, two angels, attended the wedding of Adam and Eve. They are considered the prototypical friends of the bride and groom. The groom's friends might be in charge of the ring(s). The bride's friends may be asked to hold the *ketubah* and help lift the veil when the bride sips the wine. Grandparents and siblings may also join the processional. Older participants may be seated during the ceremony.

At the conclusion of the wedding ceremony, the bride and groom walk up the aisle together, followed, in reverse order, by those who participated in the processional.

Some couples hold a rehearsal a few days before the wedding. This is not at all necessary. If the attendants arrive before the other guests, a brief rehearsal at that time should prove sufficient to create a dignified wedding processional.

Some brides and grooms fast on their wedding day until they share a sip of wine under the *ḥuppah*. The traditional feeling is that for them, this day is a kind of Yom Kippur, a day of contemplation of the past and a looking forward to the future. It is the finale of one kind of life and the prelude to another. Just as fasting on Yom Kippur is meant to cleanse the soul, so too, abstaining from food on one's wedding day symbolizes the cleansing of all one's past misdeeds and the beginning of a new life.

The Wedding Ceremony

The Jewish wedding ceremony began to take its present form in the eleventh century. Prior to that time, marriage was accomplished in two separate rituals which took place approximately a year apart.

The first ritual was a betrothal ceremony known as *erusin*. It differed from the modern concept of engagement: A formal bill of divorce was required if *erusin* was broken. After the betrothal ceremony, the couple set their wedding date. The bride returned to her father's house for a period of about one year. This interval allowed the groom time to learn a trade so that he would be prepared to support his family.

The second ritual was *nisuin:* the formal wedding ceremony.

Over time, the *erusin* and *nisuin* ceremonies began to take place on the same day. The modern Jewish wedding ceremony still shows the seam where the two rituals were joined; the presence of two cups of wine, or in some cases one cup filled twice, is a reminder of the time when two separate occasions were celebrated.

In some European communities it was customary for the bride, as she arrived at the *ḥuppah*, to circle the groom seven times (an alternative custom was three times). The origin of this custom is unclear. Some believe that its purpose was to ward off evil spirits. Others saw the number seven as symbolic of perfection, since the world was created in seven days. Today the circling of the groom is an optional ritual rarely seen in Conservative and Reform ceremonies.

German silver Double Marriage Cup, late nineteenth century. Wedding cups were often commissioned for use during the wedding ceremony.

Most rabbis begin the formal wedding ceremony by welcoming the bride and groom and the assembled guests. This is followed by a prayer for God's blessing:

May you who are here be blessed in the name of Adonai.

Wine is always associated with Jewish celebrations. In Orthodox and Conservative wedding ceremonies it is customary to use two cups of wine. Reform ceremonies often have a single cup of wine. The cups are placed on a small table under the *ḥuppah*. The *erusin* is celebrated with two blessings:

Blessed are You, Adonai our God, Ruler of the world,
who creates the fruit of the vine.

This is followed by another blessing, thanking God for making the couple holy by sanctifying marriage:

Blessed are You, Adonai our God, Ruler of the world,
who hallows Your people Israel with the ḥuppah and the
rites of matrimony.

The bride and groom now drink from the first cup of wine.

The groom then places the ring on his bride's right index finger. There are several explanations for the selection of this finger. Some ascribe a direct lifeline from it to the heart. Others explain that this is the finger that points to heaven, the source of all. Still others more practically assert that this finger is not generally accustomed to receiving a ring, and so its placement is not likely to be unintentional. Following the ceremony, the ring may be moved to the more usual "ring finger." Some rabbis have the ring placed directly on the finger where it will be normally.

As the groom places the ring on his bride's finger, he recites the traditional words of consecration:

By this ring you are consecrated to me as my wife
in accordance with the Law of Moses and the people of Israel.

In a double ring ceremony, the bride then gives her groom a ring and might recite:

By this ring you are consecrated to me as my husband
in accordance with the Law of Moses and the people of Israel.

or

I am my beloved's and my beloved is mine.

Some couples add a favorite poem or a personal statement during the exchange of rings. You might discuss this possibility with your rabbi.

The ring ceremony completes the first part of the wedding ceremony.

There are no formal vows in the Jewish wedding liturgy. However, some rabbis do include vows immediately following the exchange of rings:

Do you, _____, take _____, to be your
husband/wife, promising to protect and cherish him/her, whether
in good fortune or in adversity, and to seek together a life hallowed
by the faith of Israel?

Some Conservative and Reform rabbis may permit the recitation of your own written vows during this part of the ceremony.

The rabbi now reads either all or a portion of the *ketubah*. It is then given to the groom, who gives it to his bride. The bride, who will have permanent possession of the document, may give it to her parents or to an attendant for temporary safe-keeping.

After the *ketubah* reading, some rabbis make a personal statement to the bride and groom. Others may deliver a brief message about marriage in general. You may wish to discuss the content of this presentation with your rabbi, perhaps sharing personal anecdotes or other information that might be included.

The recitation of the Seven Blessings of Marriage (*Sheva Brakhot*) follows. The blessings are usually recited by the rabbi or cantor. Sometimes close friends or relatives of the bride and groom are invited to recite the blessings. Each blessing can be followed by a personal wish for the bride and groom.

SHEVA BRAKHOT—THE SEVEN BLESSINGS OF MARRIAGE

Blessed are You, Adonai our God, Ruler of the world,
who creates the fruit of the vine.

Blessed are You, Adonai our God, Ruler of the world,
who has created all things for Your glory.

Blessed are You, Adonai our God, Ruler of the world,
our Creator.

Blessed are You, Adonai our God, Ruler of the world,
who has fashioned us in Your own image, after
your own likeness, and has established through us an
enduring edifice of life. Blessed are You, Adonai,
our Creator.

May Zion, who has been made barren of her children,
soon rejoice as her children return joyfully unto her.

Blessed are You, Adonai, who causes Zion to rejoice at
the return of her children.

Bestow abundant joy to the beloved companions as
You did bestow joy upon the first man and wife in the
Garden of Eden. Blessed are You, Adonai, who bestows
joy upon groom and bride.

Blessed are You, Adonai our God, Ruler of the world,
who has created joy and gladness, a groom and his bride,
mirth and exultation, dancing and jubilation, love
and harmony, peace and companionship. O Adonai our God,
may there soon be heard again in the cities of Judah
and in the streets of Jerusalem glad and joyous voices,
the voices of groom and bride, the jubilant voices
of those joined in marriage under the huppah, the voices
of young people feasting and singing. Blessed are You,
Adonai, who causes the groom to rejoice with his bride.

The bride and groom now drink from the second cup of wine.

Some rabbis end the wedding ceremony with the official pronouncement: "By the power vested in me . . . you are now husband and wife." Others bless the bride and groom with the threefold priestly benediction:

> *May Adonai bless you and keep you.*
> *May Adonai show you favor and be gracious unto you.*
> *May Adonai show you kindness and give you peace.*

At this point the groom smashes a wrapped glass with his foot. This ancient cus-

tom has been given a variety of interpretations. One, dating back to talmudic times, speaks of Rabbi Mar de-Rabina, who felt that his disciples had become too frivolous at the wedding of his son. He grabbed a costly glass and threw it to the ground. This act had a sobering effect on the guests. His message was that where there is celebration, there should also be awe and trembling. A related interpretation sees the breaking of the glass as a reminder of the destruction of the Temple in Jerusalem.

This somber reflection lasts for just an instant. Shouts of *mazal tov* greet the sound of shattered glass. Music and spontaneous hand clapping greet the newly married couple as they leave the *ḥuppah*.

Following the recessional, the bride and groom spend a few moments alone. This custom is called *yiḥud* and began in ancient times when the groom brought his bride to his tent to consummate the marriage. It is customary for the bride and groom to break their fast during *yiḥud*, sharing their first food as husband and wife.

After your wedding ceremony, do share a few moments alone together before returning to greet your guests. These precious minutes can be memorable and lasting. The *yiḥud* experience will give you a peaceful time for shared reflection. The bride's room or the rabbi's study will be made available to you.

The *nisuin* are now complete.

After the Ceremony

The reception following the wedding ceremony is truly a *simḥah*, an occasion of great joy. The celebration is so important in Jewish tradition that the Talmud tells us even the study of Torah must be interrupted to bring joy and honor to newlyweds.

At the wedding feast, singing, dancing, and merrymaking are the rule. The bride and groom are often lifted on chairs and carried around the room. It is a religious commandment, a *mitzvah*, to rejoice with the bride and groom.

The wedding reception is traditionally ended with the recitation of the Grace after Meals, *Birkat Ha-Mazon*. In the special Grace for weddings, the seven blessings recited under the *ḥuppah* are recited once again. Friends of the bride and groom can be honored with the recitation of selected blessings. Two cups of wine are then poured together into a third cup. The bride and groom both drink from this cup in symbolic acceptance of the joining of the streams of their lives.

It is nice to remember the less fortunate at times of celebration. You might arrange to share your flowers with hospital patients and leftover foods with the needy in your community.

························■························

"Go eat your bread with gladness

and drink your wine with a joyous heart."

·········■·········

ECCLESIASTES 9:7

In days gone by, brides and grooms spent the first week of married life surrounded by friends and relatives who fed and entertained them. This custom probably originated with the biblical seven-day banquet prepared by Laban for Jacob and Leah. Although more traditional couples still observe this custom, the honeymoon trip usually displaces it.

Since biblical times, the special status of a bride and groom lasted for one complete year. The Book of Deuteronomy informs us: "When a man takes a wife, he shall be deferred from military duty. . . . He shall be free in his house one year and shall cheer his wife whom he has taken." (24:5) The first year of every marriage presents a host of decisions and adjustments, bringing with them tension and stress. Judaism's advice to newlyweds is clearly to stay at home and learn to live with one another.

When you marry, you become the newest Jewish family in your community. Jewish history begins with the family; many stories in the Bible deal with family histories. There are the examples of the filial obedience of Isaac, the love of Jacob for Rachel, the bond of friendship between Ruth and her mother-in-law Naomi. These and many others give testimony to family affection and the unique quality of Jewish family life.

Traditionally an important goal of every Jewish family is to create an atmosphere of peace, *shalom bayit*. A Jewish home nurtures and promotes togetherness, cooperation, and respect.

As a Jewish family, you can enrich your life with the symbolic objects and ritual acts of Judaism. Together you can celebrate the holy days of the Jewish year as well as the personal life-cycle events of your family. May you have a lifetime together filled with joyous celebration!

On the Birth of a Baby

"The mitzvah of being fruitful and multiplying

exists so that the earth will be settled.

And it is a great mitzvah . . .

because of it, all the others exist."

SEFER HINNUKH, BEREISHIT

You're Expecting a Baby!

Nothing changes one's life as much as the experience of becoming a parent. The "before child" world of personal quiet time and freedom of movement is quickly replaced by the serious and seemingly endless responsibility of caring for a human being totally dependent on you for every need.

Before we had children, people tried to describe the experience to us, to let us know what to expect. We learned how to count through contractions, how to diaper and burp. We read books on fetal development and discussed the ways in which our relationship would become strained. But despite the best efforts, we were not entirely prepared for what was to come, for a birth, the creation of a new family unit, is an intensely emotional experience, one that can be truly understood only as it occurs. One thing is certain: Life is never quite the same again.

Imagine for a moment a scene at the beach in summer. Children romp in the ocean and dig in the sand. Parents are unable to relax fully, for they have to make sure that their children don't eat sand or drown in the waves. Anyone would long for the "pre-child" days, days of lying on a blanket, listening to the surf, and reading a book. Yet, it is the parents who are the lucky ones. They are the ones who experience the joys and pleasures of play, along with their children. They are the ones who have the opportunity to be children once more, to grow up all over again, to feel life's surprises as though they were new.

For Jewish parents, the experience goes even deeper, for just as we strive to perpetuate ourselves personally, we as a people have always been driven to perpetuate Torah. What is Torah without children to receive it? What is Judaism without the links of the generations? Our children not only bring us to life, they bring our Judaism to life.

On two counts, then, we wish you a hearty *mazal tav:* for yourself, for you will have the wonderful opportunity to grow up all over again with someone new and beautiful to love; and for the Jewish people, whose love of God and Torah will continue for yet another generation.

We hope that this guide will give you food for thought as the birth of your new baby draws near. We have tried to be mainstream in our presentation, but as we all know, for every Jew there are at least two options. Issues of Jewish law and denominationalism are not fully explored here, and in some areas there is a wider range of opinion and practice than what is presented. If you wish further information on any of these topics, or if you have additional questions, you should consult your rabbi.

With each new experience our Jewish knowledge grows. Often it is our children who force us closer to our faith. They do so even before they are born!

Rabbi Douglas Weber
Jessica Brodsky Weber

Preparing for Your Baby

What the Sages Understood About Gestation

The Rabbis of the Talmud offer us advice and information on a myriad of topics. Their advice was based on observation, on the spiritual and legal framework of the tradition, and on the latest scientific data of their day. One of these topics is gestation, and while the Rabbis were certainly not experts in the area, they showed great interest in it and devoted much space to it in the Talmud. Their stories and thoughts on the subject are not to be taken in the same way as information from prenatal and birth classes. They do, however, represent a spiritual look at our struggle to understand how life comes about. In this sense, the Rabbis offer us wisdom valid in any age.

"For this child I prayed. . ."

I SAMUEL 1:27

One talmudic midrash explains that there are three partners in the creation of a child: the father, the mother, and God. The father provides the white matter, such as the bones, sinews, nails, brain, and the whites of the eyes. The mother provides the red matter which forms the flesh, the hair, the blood, the skin, and the dark of the eyes. God offers the spirit, the breath, the beauty of the features, and the ability to see, hear, think, speak, and walk.

According to another midrash, at conception God forces a soul to enter the new being. The soul is reluctant to do so, for it does not want to give up its freedom for a stay on earth. Yet it has no choice. In utero a light burns over the new child's head, enabling it to see from one end of the earth to the other. The child has complete knowledge of Torah and has full understanding of life and death. Just before birth, the child is touched by an angel, causing her to forget this infinite wisdom. Folklore tells us that the indentation of the upper lip is the permanent sign of that angel's touch.

Folk Customs

The months before a child's birth are filled with excitement and expectation. Parents are eager to buy the crib and the car seat and the baby clothes and to set up the nursery. Friends want to plan a baby shower to help expectant parents make everything for the new arrival.

Many Jews, however, refrain from such preparations, preferring to wait until after the baby is born to make their home physically ready for the baby. This superstition (or *bubeh meiseh*) originally arose from a desire, in times past, to ward off demons and bad luck. Many Jewish parents today see a certain logic in delaying

Pendant amulet. Istanbul, nineteenth century.
For protection against harm.

celebration until there is something to celebrate: a new baby, home with Mom and Dad. Many baby stores, recognizing this reluctance, will hold items chosen in advance until after the baby's birth, and deliver them in time to welcome everyone home from the hospital.

Folk customs surrounding birth are numerous in every culture. Jews have picked up various beliefs from our neighbors around the world and have made them our own. Placing the circumcision knife under the pillow of the mother the night before the *brit*, to protect her from demons, follows similar customs in other cultures where weapons of iron are kept near newborns. Amulets to ward off evil spirits are used in many traditions, but Jewish amulets contain verses from the Psalms, especially the verse, "The sun shall not smite thee by day, neither the moon by night" (21:6).

There are many other folk customs, some of which you might know from your own family. Here are a few:

1. The custom of not announcing a child's name until the circumcision or naming ceremony comes from the talmudic concept that the baby is not entirely viable until the eighth day.

2. Garlic and red ribbons were placed on the baby's crib to protect it from the evil eye, or demons. Lilith, one demon in particular, is suspected of stealing small children for herself, since, as legend has it, she is forever bitter about her own inability to bear children.

3. Yemenite Jews place sweets under the bed of the new mother to occupy the evil spirits and to draw attention away from the baby.

4. During difficult labor, Ashkenazi Jews would sometimes put a Torah binder around the belly of the woman or put the keys to the synagogue in her hands.

5. In ancient Israel it was customary to plant a tree for the new baby.

Some people even create their own customs during pregnancy by responding to charity solicitations or engaging in other philanthropic activity just to feel safe. Despite our sophisticated attitudes and modern science and technology, to discard our folk customs entirely would be to assume that we have total control over our lives and our environment. So, even if we don't want garlic on the crib, and even if we believe that candy under the bed will bring bugs, we can always give extra *tzedakah*. That never hurts!

Choosing a Name for the Baby

Choosing names can be a wonderful experience. To select for sound and tone, for historical significance and meaning, an aspect of human beings that they will carry with them all their lives, is a creative opportunity. When we select a name, we think of what we wish that child to be like. We think of loved ones no longer with us whose examples we wish them to follow. We send our children out into the world with the best names we can offer, and we hope that, as adults, they will like our choices.

Jewish names come from several sources. Traditionally, the first source has always been the Bible. The names of the righteous, brave, and generous personages in the Scriptures have always been popular.

....

"A fair name is better than a precious balm."

....

ECCLESIASTES.

A recent trend has been toward modern Hebrew names, which include aspects of nature as well as other picturesque nouns and verbs. These are used more frequently for girls, since the Bible is a much richer source of male names. There are several Jewish name dictionaries that offer many possibilities.

A third source of Jewish names has always been the surrounding culture within which we live. Even the Rabbis of the Talmud are sometimes recognized with Greek names such as Antigonus and Avtalyon. Some of our names are translations of Hebrew into a vernacular, such as Moses for Moshe, or Susanne for Shoshannah. In any case, when using English names, or names in another foreign tongue, it is not traditional to choose those with a Christian connotation.

It has been a long-standing custom in the Jewish community to have a civil name along with a Jewish name. It is convenient here to bridge the gap between the two by providing an English name that has a Hebrew equivalent, such as David or Miriam. Names can also be paired by sound (e.g., Jason for Grandpa Jack) or by meaning (Bloomah, meaning flower, for Great Grandma Florence, also means flower).

In our Hebrew names we follow the ancient custom of calling ourselves by a first name plus son or daughter of our parents. For example, the biblical Jacob was called Yaakov Ben Yitzhak, or Jacob the son of Isaac. Rachel was known as Rachel Bat Laban, or Rachel the daughter of Laban. Many modern Jews now include the mother's name as well, so that both parents are represented in the child's Hebrew name.

European Ashkenazic tradition discourages the naming of a child after someone who is living. In the Sephardic tradition, however, naming children after living persons is permissible and common, though these rarely include parents.

Formal Hebrew names are given either at the *brit milah* or at the naming ceremony. We are known by these names within the Jewish community, using them when we are called to the Torah and during life-cycle events. When we are called to the Torah as a Bar/Bat Mitzvah, when we recite marriage vows under the *huppah*, or when we are eulogized, it is by our Hebrew name that we are known.

It is interesting to note that Jews did not always have last names. Surnames were not necessary when Jews lived in small towns and had little contact with the outside world. Someone could have been called Chaim ben Moshe all his life, never needing a last name. Or he could have been called Chaim the Baker, based on his profession. About 200 years ago European countries began requiring Jews to take last names and to register them officially.

Jews most often created their last names from their professions or from the names of their towns and cities. The name Weber is German for "weaver," and the name Brodsky means "son of Brod," a Polish town. Some names came from personal characteristics such as Gross, Weiss, and Schwartz. These names soon took root and were passed from generation to generation. They became the names that we now know as "Jewish" names, although we should keep in mind that in terms of Jewish history they aren't old at all.

Blessings on the Birth of a Baby

Our tradition offers us a wide vocabulary of blessings. In reciting them, we acknowledge God's role in providing our food, our health, the beauties of nature, the Torah, our holidays, and for enabling us to reach landmark events in our lives. We have blessings to mark the small, simple moments as well as the less frequent but special times—words of praise that turn these experiences into holy events. Blessings teach us to sanctify time and ensure that we will not take anything for granted.

Most blessings begin with the same formula, *"Barukh atah, Adonai Eloheinu, melekh ha-olam . . ."* (Blessed are you, Adonai our God, Ruler of the world . . .), and conclude with the appropriate phrase for the situation. Some are long, like the five-paragraph blessing we recite after reading the *haftarah*, and some are simple, like the single sentence we say over wine.

It is odd, therefore, considering the importance we place on blessings within our tradition, that there is no specific blessing or ritual to mark the moment of birth. Perhaps if the Rabbis had been the ones actually giving birth, a customary blessing would have been recorded. Since none has, many women feel that it is time to create this new ritual.

Blu Greenberg, a well-known voice among liberal Orthodox women, suggests that parents recite the same blessing that is used upon hearing any good news. It goes as follows: *"Barukh atah, Adonai Eloheinu, melekh ha-olam, ha-tov vuha-meytiv"*— "Blessed are You, Adonai our God, Ruler of the world who is good and does good."

The book *Gates of Mitzvah*, published by the Reform Movement, cites the *Sheheḥeyanu* blessing as one that is appropriate for that occasion. This blessing is said when one has any experience for the first time: *"Barukh atah, Adonai Eloheinu, melekh ha-olam, sheheḥeyanu, v'kiyemanu, vhigiyanu lazman hazeh"*— "Blessed are you, Adonai our God, Ruler of the world, who has given us life, sustained us, and helped us to reach this special day."

The following prayer of thanksgiving has been offered within the Reconstructionist Movement: "How wonderful is this moment as we stand at the edge of the mystery of life. Our daughter/son, how small and beautiful you are. . . . Let our arms be your love cradle; our whispered prayer, your lullaby song. . . . In awe and gratitude for this precious gift of life, we celebrate our partnership in the miracle of creation."

It is certainly proper to offer a blessing of thanks at the completion of such a monumental event as a birth. By remembering to thank God, we give ourselves the opportunity to create special *kodesh*, or a holy moment in our lives, and to appreciate the grandeur of life.

Ceremony for a Son: Brit Milah

What Is a Brit Milah?

Brit (*bris* in Yiddish) is the Hebrew word for "covenant"; *milah* means "circumcision." The Torah describes a series of covenants. The universal *brit* between God and all humanity was made through Noah; the great covenant at Sinai was made with the Jewish people in particular. A critical step in this evolution is described in Genesis 17, where God commands Abraham to bear the mark of his special relationship to God in his (and his descendants') flesh.

Shrouded in prehistory, the act of removing the foreskin which covers the glans of the penis certainly existed before Abraham's time. It was practiced by a variety of ancient cultures before being invested with the overtly religious significance it took on in Judaism. Philo of Alexandria (living in Hellenistic culture and seeking to demonstrate the compatibility of Torah and reason) described *milah* as a method to safeguard cleanliness and health. Maimonides (who similarly made great efforts to harmonize Torah with the science of his day) viewed circumcision as a means to curb lust and as a symbol of sacrifice.

The importance of *milah* to Jewish survival has always been perceived by anti-Semites. The familiar Ḥanukkah story begins in 165 B.C.E. with a royal decree forbidding circumcision in an attempt to destroy Jewish distinctiveness. Three centuries later the Hadrianic persecutions focused on what Rome saw as the cornerstone of Jewish identity: study of Torah and the practice of *brit malah*. Over the millennia, Jews and their detractors have agreed on this point: without *brit milah*, the Jews as a people would not last long.

········· ◆ ·········

"Behold how gladsome is circumcision that

not even the Sabbath defers it."

········· ◆ ·········

NEDARIM 31B

Under normal circumstances, infant boys undergo the minor operation. Bleeding is usually very limited. Detailed and exact instructions on the dressing and care of the minor wound are given. Usually a complete healing takes place in a few days.

Debate continues, and surely always will, over the medical necessity or advisability of routine circumcision. Advocates of the procedure point to statistically lower

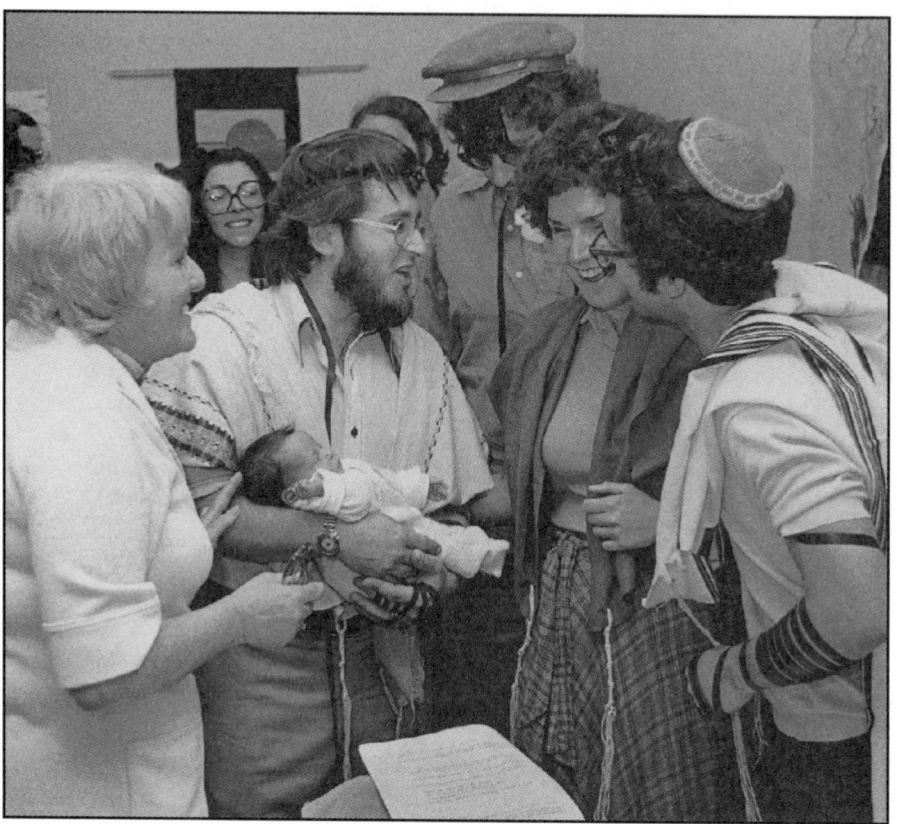

rates of cervical cancer and pelvic inflammatory disease among women whose sexual partners are circumcised. Detractors see the operation—from a strictly medical perspective—as superfluous in an age of improved hygienic conditions.

These developments highlight the essential *religious* nature of *brit malah*. As with many *mitzvot* (e.g., *kashrut*), there may be health advantages or (e.g., Shabbat) good common sense benefits. These, however, remain secondary to the purpose of *mitzvot*, which is to draw us closer to God and increase a sense of *kedushah* (sanctity) in our lives.

The true sense of *brit milah* is understood fully only when the words are joined together. All humankind enjoys a *brit* ("covenant") with God. In North America the vast majority of men have undergone circumcision. Only a Jew, however, can have a *brit milah*. Without the proper recitation of the associated blessing and the declaration by the parents that this procedure is being done so as to enter their son into an elevated relationship with God, the circumcision is merely a medical procedure.

In North America *brit malah* can be performed in either of two ways. It may be done by a physician (Jewish, if possible) in conjunction with a rabbi or other Jew who is conversant with the ritual aspects of the ceremony. The more traditional method is to employ a *mohel*, often referred to in Yiddish as "*moyl*," a ritual circumciser.

In biblical times fathers usually circumcised their own sons, but by the common era it became standard practice to employ a specialist to perform the *mitzvah* on one's behalf. To this day, the *brit milah* ceremony traditionally begins with a declaration by the father of his intention to carry out this *mitzvah*, before the *mohel* or other person appointed by him actually does the procedure on his behalf.

Mohalim (plural of *mohel*) are usually rabbis or cantors who have been trained in the specific medical procedure and religious laws pertaining to *brit milah*. Some received their training in the time-honored apprentice system, watching and assisting a master *mohel* (often their own fathers) perform hundreds of such procedures before going on their own. More often in modern times a *mohel* has been trained in a major urban teaching hospital under the guidance of both rabbis and urologists. Most *mohalim* are Orthodox, although a fair number of Conservative and other non-Orthodox rabbis have this training, often from hospital programs in Israel.

Curiously, the physicians who are most comfortable performing circumcisions are not, as one might think, urologists or pediatricians but rather obstetricians. This is so because in hospitals where male babies are routinely circumcised (unless the parents have made a request to the contrary), the procedure is done by the mother's doctor—her obstetrician.

Many parents favor using a *mohel* over a physician as a "super specialist" and prefer that the ritual take place at home in the warm company of family and friends.

That said, here are a few things to consider:

Physician or *mohel* reputation is everything. Ask your rabbi for a recommendation. Rabbis attend many such ceremonies each year. They know who is quick and competent. This is not a service to choose from the Yellow Pages!

Some physicians have special training in *brit milah*. Both the Reform and Conservative Movements have such programs in place in a few major cities. Again, your rabbi is the most trustworthy source of information in locating such a person.

If you use a *mohel* who is Orthodox and your rabbi is not, find out if the *mohel* is willing to participate with your rabbi. Some will not cooperate with non-Orthodox rabbis, though many will.

If you live in a place where there is neither a *mohel* nor Jewish physician, there are alternatives. Under such circumstances *halakhah* permits a non-Jew to do the actual cutting, as long as it is a Jew who conducts the ritual aspects (saying the blessings, naming the child, etc.). When possible, however, a Jewish circumciser should be used.

You want the best for your baby. So does the Royal Family of England, who surely can afford the best. Males of the English monarch are all circumcised, and in a country full of superb physicians, it has been long-standing tradition that the kings and princes of Great Britain are attended by none other than the Jewish Snowman family of London. Does your "prince" deserve less?

Why on the Eighth Day?

Jews often seem to disagree on just about everything, from the politics of the Middle East to basic theology. What question could one ask a member of a egalitarian *ḥavurah* in Boston, a Yemenite Jew in Israel, and the Lubavitcher Rebbe in Brooklyn and expect to receive the same answer?

Question: When does *brit milah* take place?

Answer: On the eighth day of the boy's life.

Amazing! Such unanimity! Unless there is a crucial medical reason in an individual case (such as very low birth weight), *brit milah* is always performed on the eighth day, following the instructions in the Torah: "At the age of eight days every male among you throughout the generations shall be circumcised". Genesis 17:12 and repeated in *Leviticus 12:3*. This has been our practice since we received Torah, and there has never been a good reason to change it.

So important is the custom, that a *brit milah* may—indeed, must—be held on Yom Kippur if that is the child's eighth day of life. The *Shulḥan Arukh* (the most widely known legal code) specifies that if one is a *mohel*, one may even ignore certain of the laws of mourning, even for one's father or mother, in order to attend a *brit milah*.

What if the baby is born five days earlier than expected and the grandparents already purchased their nonrefundable discount airline tickets and won't arrive until the baby is thirteen days old? What if a sister's college graduation 500 miles away is scheduled for that very day?

Judaism is not always a convenient religion. (Would it not be easier if all our holidays could come on Sundays, so we would not need to miss school or work?) We hold *brit milah* on the eighth day, as early as possible in the morning, not out of convenience, but for the same reason Abraham and Sarah did. *Brit milah* is the most tangible physical sign of our binding ourselves to God.

Jewish Godparents: Kvaterim

At the *brit milah* ceremony for boys, it is customary to appoint a *kvater* (a man) and a *kvaterin* (a woman) whose ritual role is to bring the child into the room for circumcision. In this manner, the *kvater* and *kvaterin* are honored at the *brit milah*. These people fill the role of "godparents" in Judaism.

Toward the end of the ceremony all the assembled pray together that the child will enter a life of "Torah, marriage, and good deeds." In case of the death or incapacity of both parents, the *kvaterim* (plural, including both godfather and godmother) are charged with the responsibility to see that the child enters a life of Torah, marriage, and good deeds. At the ceremony, therefore, you are publicly appointing the moral guardians of your child. In this light, the birth of children certainly calls for an update of one's legal will, even if you have few financial assets. For only via a legally drawn will can you be assured of the guardianship of your children, should both parents die while they are minors.

In addition to the *kvaterim*, who are responsible for nurturing, educating, and morally guiding a child in case they are needed, it is also traditional to appoint a *sandak*. The best translation of this word is "man holding a baby while it is being circumcised." Sometimes the word is also translated as "godfather," but this fails to convey the true meaning.

The *sandak* is most often the boy's paternal grandfather or a great-grandfather. Some families have the paternal act as *sandak* for one child, and the maternal

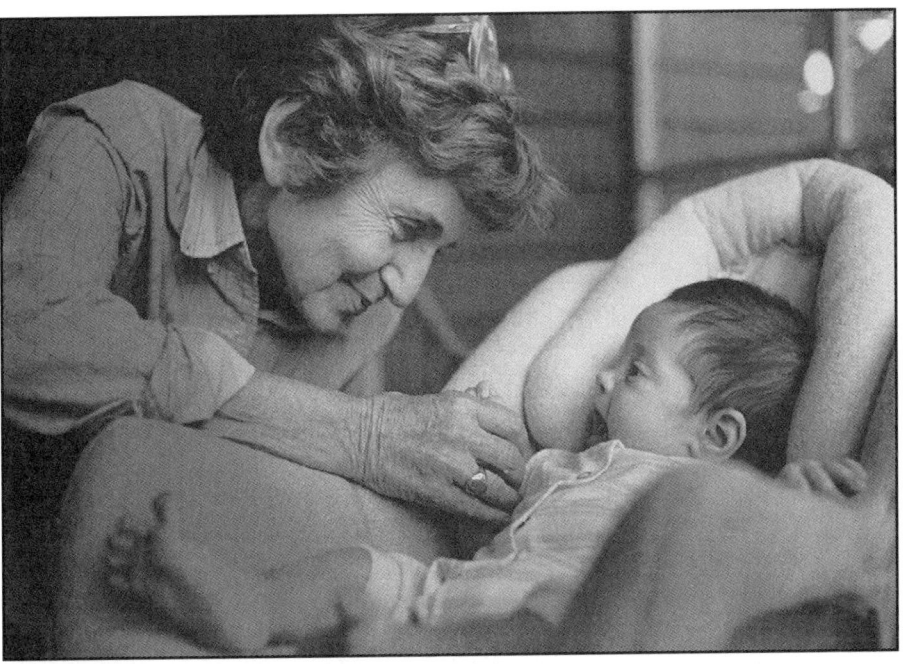

grandfather do so for a second or third child. While there are no hard and fast rules, no one should serve as a *sandak* more than once.

The role of the *sandak*, other than to hold the baby at the ceremony, is to act as an elder, a sage, a voice of wisdom born of years. It is a great honor to be appointed *sandak*.

The roles assigned to "godparents" are more than honorific. Talk to your brothers, sisters, or friends before springing this decision upon them. Are they truly the kind of people you can fully trust with Jewishly educating and raising your child? To be true to the essence of Judaism, the decision of whom to appoint to these roles should be made with deliberation, introspection, honesty, and a bit of prayer.

Preparing for the Brit

First and foremost, you need to have on hand whatever your doctor or *mohel* recommends for care of the small wound created by the circumcision itself. This usually consists of some sterile gauze pads and an antiseptic ointment.

The *mohel* may examine the baby a few days before the *brit milah* takes place to ascertain that the baby is large and healthy enough to undergo the procedure. In addition, he will provide a list of ritual and medical items needed for the ceremony. This visit will give you the opportunity to ask questions and alleviate some of the natural anxiety we all feel, particularly with our first sons.

If your baby is given a pacifier, or if you bottle-feed him, make sure to have one on hand, as sucking gives infants a great sense of comfort. Mothers who breast-feed will want to time feedings that day so that the baby will be able to nurse immediately after the *brit milah*.

The following is a list of required ritual items:

1. A place for the circumcision to take place (a very stable table).
2. A pillow or cushion for the baby to lie on.
3. A chair to be left empty which will be designated during the ceremony as "the chair of Elijah."
4. A *tallit*. Some drape the *tallit* over Elijah's chair; others place the baby on it.
5. A *Kiddush* cup of wine. Sweet kosher wine is traditional. Your baby will be drinking a drop or two of it, so old-fashioned sweet wine is best. (If any of the major participants is an alcoholic, it is perfectly acceptable to use kosher grape juice instead.)
6. Photocopies of any responsive readings or prayers you wish guests to recite.
7. If you hold a traditional *seudat mitzvah* (a full meal) afterwards, you may want to provide copies of *Birkat Ha-Mazon* (the blessing after the meal, which has specific additions for the *brit milah*).
8. A ḥallah.

One thing you don't need for *brit milah* is printed invitations. Since a *brit milah*, when done the proper day, comes so soon after the birth, there is little time to send written invitations.

By tradition, it is considered such an important *mitzvah* to attend a *brit milah* that the custom is simply to tell guests, "The *bris* will be Thursday at 10 o'clock at our house." For those unfamiliar with the custom of not overtly inviting guests, adding the words, "We hope you can come," provides a welcoming gesture.

"Abraham took Ishmael, his son,

and all that were born in his house,

and circumcised the flesh of their

foreskin on the selfsame day."

GENESIS 17:23

Probably the most important preparation you need to do for the *brit* ceremony is psychological. If this is your first baby, you are experiencing a sudden loss of privacy and free time now that this attention-demanding, 24-hour-a-day visitor is making his home with you. Some people fear their first child's *bris* as overwhelming, and indeed it can feel that way. Part of the loveliness of our heritage as Jews is that the many friends and family who attend the *brit milah* help to diffuse the tension and anxiety we naturally feel.

Keep this in mind: babies circumcised in hospitals undergo the procedure alone, in a sterile, friendless environment, and afterwards cry themselves to sleep in solitary basinettes. Jewish babies are given wine to drink, are cuddled before, during, and after the procedure, with their parents and dear ones feeling their discomfort with them. In a sense, the *brit milah* is a paradigm of all Jewish life, as we share each other's pain and joy together as a community. Having a large circle of fellow Jews to rejoice and cry with you is bound to be helpful.

The Brit Milah *Ceremony*

The *brit milah* ritual is rather brief. Most often it takes place at home. Though not essential, it is customary to have at least a *minyan* (a quorum of ten) on hand. Some parents find it more relaxing to hold the ceremony at a place other than their own home (e.g., synagogue or grandparents' house).

A table is set aside for the procedure, with a pillow on it, and a chair is set aside which will be designated during the ceremony as *kisey shel Eliyahu*—"the chair of Elijah." (The prophet Elijah "visits" not only at the Passover *seder* but at all *brit milah* ceremonies as well.)

The *brit milah* ceremony begins when the baby boy is brought into the room by the *kvaterim*. All present stand and say, "*Barukh ha-bah*," which means "Welcome! Blessed is he who is about to enter the covenant!" The father or both parents may be called upon to read a prayer stating that this circumcision is specifically performed for the sake of entering their son into the covenant, and delegating to the *mohel* or physician the task of actually performing the *mitzvah*.

After the baby has been placed on the pillow (or, in traditional circles, on the lap of the *sandak*), the rabbi, *mohel*, or other officiant will usually explain the significance of the ceremony, adding a *dvar Torah* (literally "a word or two of Torah") to emphasize the religious nature of the gathering. The chair of Elijah is then designated, and his presence invoked. Sometimes the infant is placed on Elijah's chair for a moment before being returned to the place where the circumcision will be performed.

At this point *mohalim*, and some physicians, will apply a clamp which draws back and holds the foreskin. This usually provokes the child to cry, often more than the incision itself. We have seen many *mohalim* do the procedure without any such clamps, however. Some use topical anesthetics, though many Orthodox circumcisers will not do so on *halakhic* (legal) grounds. There is debate on the matter.

With the *sandak* holding the baby so that he cannot move, the officiant then pronounces the blessing: "We praise You, Eternal God for making our lives holy with *mitzvot* and commanding us concerning circumcision." The circumcision is then performed; the procedure itself takes just a few seconds. After the circumcision is completed, the father (or in some places both parents) recite a blessing praising God "for having bidden us to enter our son into the covenant of Abraham our father."

At this point all present say, "*Keshem shenichnas labrit, ken yikanes l'Torah, u'lechupah, u'l'maasim tovim.* As he has entered the covenant, so too may he enter a life of Torah, marriage, and good deeds.

The officiant then recites a long blessing over a cup of wine; it includes a formal naming of the baby and a petition that he may grow to learn the full meaning of the covenant into which he has been brought. It is traditional to dip a finger or bit

Carved beechwood circumcision chair.

Austria, 1791

of gauze into the wine to give the baby some to drink. (Some even do so during the circumcision, to help calm the baby.) Often the rabbi or *mohel* will take a moment to explain the meaning of the baby's Hebrew name and whether he is being named after a certain person. If the baby was not born to a halakhically Jewish mother, many rabbis or *mohalim* will take the opportunity to recite a formula overtly stating that this is done *l'shem gerut*, that is, "for the sake of conversion." Doing so, and later visiting the *mikveh*, will make the child's identity as a Jew acceptable to all streams of Judaism.

At the conclusion of the ceremony, special prayers are said on behalf of the infant. The traditional blessing is recited: "May God bless you and keep you. May God smile upon you and be gracious to you. May God look well upon you and grant you *shalom* (peace, or better, "wholeness"). Sometimes a few psalms are added. In traditional circles, when a *minyan* is present, the entire assembly recites the *Alenu* prayer.

Of all the life-cycle events, differences in customs of the various streams of Judaism are minimal concerning circumcision. By and large, *brit milah* is psychodynamically highly charged to begin with, and most people find adding very much to the ancient rite superfluous and artificial. It is precisely at moments such as these that the reassurance we feel in conducting ourselves in time-hallowed ways is strongest.

Celebration: Seudat Mitzvah

The festive meal after any happy life-cycle event is called *seudat mitzvah*.

There is great latitude in planning a *seudat mitzvah*. When planning the menu, consider *kashrut* so that all the guests, both observant and not, can enjoy the meal. Smoked fish such as lox, creamed herring, whitefish, salads, and the like are popular. *Nahit* (cold, salted chickpeas) are also common at a *brit*, as are alcoholic beverages. It is customary for guests to offer a "*l'chayim!*" (a toast, "to life!"). Lifting a *schnapps* or two at a *bris* has been a healthy manifestation of the Jewish propensity toward moderation in all things. As Ecclesiastes tells us, "To everything there is a season." That said, make sure that nonalcoholic beverages are available for guests with medical or chemical dependency problems. Proper hospitality these days means thinking ahead and providing for such special needs.

One of the traditional aspects of a *brit milah* is that, at the conclusion of the festivities, a special version of *Birkat Ha-Mazon* (blessing after the meal) is recited. Some people purchase or borrow special *benchers* (pamphlets with the special prayers printed inside) for the occasion. The traditional *halakhah* is that one recites the *Birkat Ha-Mazon* only after a meal that includes bread and would therefore begin with the *Motzi* blessing. If it is not your custom to recite *Birkat Ha-Mazon*, it is still perfectly natural to begin the festivities with *Ha-Motzi* over hallah.

One of the blessings in the *Birkat Ha-Mazon* refers to "*shulhan zeh sh'akhalnu alay*," "this table, upon which we have eaten." Traditionally, this has been taken to mean that the festive meal is a full-scale sit-down affair. And, indeed, many people find that after they include all the proper friends and relatives, they have a full-scale celebration on their hands. This need not happen. A baby party can be lovely even when kept simple. Keep in mind that your guests are not expecting to attend a wedding or Bar Mitzvah! Simplicity reinforces the real message that the party should convey, that this is a *seudat mitzvah*. Keep in mind that your table, even if you are serving a simple buffet, is like the altar in the sanctuary, and with that sentiment everything else will fall into place. Families are encouraged to share their good fortune with others in need through an act of *tzedakah*.

Is an Uncircumcised Baby Still a Jew?

According to traditional Jewish law (*halakhah*), a baby born to a Jewish mother is considered a Jew whether or not he is circumcised. Failure of the parents to perform the *mitzvah* of *brit milah* does not alter the child's identity as a Jew.

Reform and Reconstructionist Judaism affirm "patrilineal descent." Children are extended a presumption of Jewish identity if either mother *or* father is a Jew when a declaration is made that the child is to be raised unambiguously as a Jew. A child's identity is affirmed by the timely performance of the customary life-cycle *mitzvot*, of which, for a male, *brit milah* is primary.

Traditionally, an uncircumcised male (called a *arel*) is considered a Jew, but such men are often not extended certain ritual honors, such as being called to the Torah or asked to lead the congregation in prayer. Rabbinic literature is rather complex on this matter, with some authorities denying the right of *Sheva Brakhot* (the seven benedictions) to an uncircumcised groom, though none deny such a man the right

Embroidered cushion for circumcision bench.

Germany, 1729

to a Jewish wedding per se. Opinions in this century, even among some major Reform authorities, have upheld the correctness of maintaining such distinctions.

Brit milah is a unique *mitzvah*. Unlike the many *mitzvot* we choose for ourselves, no one asks an eight-day-old infant his opinion on the matter. The commandment is incumbent on the father, and failure to arrange for the timely entry of one's son into the covenant is universally seen as shirking a basic responsibility. If the father does not do so, then the mother ought to see to the *brit milah* herself. In Exodus 4:24–26 we read a rather cryptic, enigmatic tale. Moses, for a reason we do not know, has neglected to circumcise his son, and his wife Zipporah takes matters into her own hands. She *personally* performs the act (at the time done with a flint knife) and flings the foreskin at Moses, chastising him bitterly.

There have been various periods in Jewish history when circumcision was neglected. The Bible describes how the generation that had wandered in the desert had not been circumcised; thus—before setting out into the Promised Land—all the males were circumcised in a mass act of community purification (Joshua 5:2–9). Later, in a period of Greek cultural influence in Israel, some Jewish men even sought to "reverse" their circumcisions through painful building up of scar tissue so as to be more at home in the gymnasia.

In periods of severe persecution, especially during the Inquisition in Spain and the Holocaust in Europe, many Jewish parents sought to shield their sons from being known as Jews by withholding *brit milah*. Almost all modern rabbis have at some time needed to counsel men born in the Soviet Union or Eastern European countries after World War II who were not circumcised at birth for fear of another Holocaust.

Parents unswayed by arguments for circumcision from tradition ought at least to keep these questions in mind:

If the father is circumcised, what will the psychological impact be when the son recognizes that he is substantially *different* from his own father?

What would happen if your son grew up to be religiously more traditional than his parents? *Halakhah* (traditional Jewish law) is clear: once past the age of 13, the *mitzvah* becomes incumbent upon the son himself. Circumcision later in life is far more serious and painful than the simple, relatively easy procedure done on the eighth day of life.

What would be the son's feelings when, in summer camp or other situations where children see one another naked, he discovers that he is quite unlike all the other Jewish boys he knows? How can he grow up to feel like a Jew if he lacks this basic mark of the covenant?

A decision not to circumcise one's son, though not affecting his status as a Jew, may pose social problems for him later in life, since circumcision is such a revered universal practice among Jews. Such a decision ought not be made lightly.

Ceremony for a Daughter: Brit Ha-Bat

Celebrating Our Daughters

Until the modern era, it was considered a great disability to be born female. Women were in little control of their own lives, had little control over property, had few ritual honors in houses of worship, and had little access to political power. No wonder the traditional *siddur* calls for men to recite a blessing every morning that praises God "for not having made me a woman." Women—in seeming resignation to the Divine will—simply recite, "Praised be God, who has made me what I am."

Because daughters were seen as financial liabilities, there was, for most of Jewish history, much more subdued rejoicing at the birth of a girl. Daughters, unlike sons, would not perpetuate family names and would not have the economic earning capacity as adults to support elderly parents. No wonder, then, that in Jewish (and most non-Jewish) traditions, premodern societies were much less jubilant concerning the birth of girls. To this day, the birth of a daughter is often marked simply by the father's being called to the Torah on the *Shabbat* after the birth. A special prayer may be recited on the daughter's behalf, and her Jewish name is announced to the community. The family may sponsor a *kiddush* for the congregation. By and large, that was universal Jewish custom until the modern era.

"Classical" Reform Judaism distinguished itself a century ago by recognizing the birth of daughters as significant events. The Reform custom was, and still is in many locales, to call both parents to the *bimah* on a Friday evening soon after the birth of a baby (boy or girl) and to invoke God's blessings on the child and her parents. A formal naming would then take place followed by the presentation of a certificate. In many Reform, Conservative, and Reconstructionist congregations these days it is customary to bring the baby girl into the synagogue for a similar ceremony, after which the rabbi might pronounce the traditional priestly blessing (the same one that is recited at the *brit* for boys).

In an effort to mark fully the complete equality of boys and girls in our era, many non-Orthodox families conduct a ceremony closely related to the *brit milah* ceremony for boys, adapted of course for girls. In addition to the more conventional "Naming Ceremony," the New Union Home Prayerbook (Reform) includes a "Covenant of Life" ceremony for girls, to be conducted in the home on the eighth day of life. The recently printed *Rabbi's Manual* (also Reform) includes a ceremony called "*hakhnasat bat la-brit*—Covenant Service for a Daughter"—that even more closely parallels the *brit milah* ceremony. The Reconstructionist movement offers a *Brit B'not Yisrael* ritual performed in the synagogue on Shabbat morning or at home on Saturday afternoon.

Kiddush cup.

At present, there are literally dozens of highly personalized ceremonies circulating within the non-Orthodox community. Here are some elements you might include if you design your own ceremony:

1. Lighting candles, with or without an innovative blessing, perhaps "We Praise You Adonai, Eternal God, for enriching our lives with *mitzvot* and causing us to enter our daughter into the covenant of the Jewish people."

2. Appointing a chair for Elijah.

3. Appointing *kvaterim* (godparents) in the same manner as with boys.

4. Some people, in an attempt to make the ceremony as analogous as possible to *brit milah*, search for some tactile act to perform at this moment. You might consider these:

   Have the officiant wash the baby girl's feet, recalling the biblical custom of foot-washing as a sign of hospitality and welcome. In this way, a *sandak* can also be involved.

   Have the officiant rub a small amount of olive oil on your daughter's forehead, recalling the biblical image of anointing.

   Have the officiant wrap your baby in a *tallit*.

Have the officiant physically place an object of Jewish significance into your daughter's hand, signifying in a ritual manner her capacity to perform *mitzvot*. This might be a Bible or a candlestick which you hope one day she may use to light Shabbat candles.

5. Include a formal naming at which your daughter's Hebrew name is announced and the significance explained. Some people also follow the custom of making an acrostic of the name using Psalm 119 (each verse begins with a different Hebrew letter in alphabetical order). If you are capable or know someone who does Hebrew calligraphy, this can be a splendid concrete reminder of the day.

6. Include a *kiddush* over wine, adding *Sheheheyanu*, the blessing for happy occasions. He who recites the blessings drinks first, then shares the wine with the newborn and her parents.

Most rabbis are quite willing and even eager to help you design a creative, original ritual for your own daughter, or to officiate using one of the new standard liturgies. Be sure to discuss this matter with your rabbi. Home-based celebrations for girls can provide an opportunity for your own Jewish learning and commitment to grow. Take it as the pleasant, creative challenge it can be, and your *simhat ha-bat* (rejoicing over a new daughter) can be a wonderful and memorable occasion.

When to Have the Ceremony

Simhat ha-bat, hakhnasat bat la-brit, and other neologisms for the ceremonies modern Jews have created to welcome their daughters into the covenant have this in common: since they are not required by traditional *halakhah*, there is great flexibility in when they can be held. They are not, traditionally, a *mitzvah she'ha-zman geramah*, "a commandment for which the time of performance is fixed." Some of the available liturgies are specifically worded to refer to the eighth day. Take care when discussing your plans with your rabbi so that the appropriate liturgy will be used.

Many people feel rather strongly that such ceremonies for girls should be timed in the same manner as the *brit milah* for boys, to stress the equality of the sexes. Doing this may mean holding the ceremony on Shabbat or holidays (if that is the eighth day of a girl's life). Keep in mind that there is leeway here. *Brit milah* takes precedence over any other scheduled event or activity. Since there are no such traditional strictures concerning ceremonies for girls, greater latitude might be extended in setting a time and place for the ceremony.

One possibility is to follow the paradigm suggested by *pidyon ha-ben* for firstborn sons. That ritual takes place any time after the thirtieth day of life, and concern for Shabbat and other family members' schedules are legitimate reason for a slight delay. You might also find that a full month after your daughter's birth you will have more energy to plan a celebration at a more leisurely pace.

Whatever route you choose, the celebration for your new daughter should not be unduly delayed; it ought to be done when your daughter is still a young infant. In keeping with the sentiment of *brit milah* for boys, we do not ask our children if they want to enter the covenant; we make this decision for them. With effort and a bit of *mazal,* your children will affirm your decision at *Bar* or *Bat Mitzvah,* at Confirmation or even later in life, but the initial act of entering the covenant is a duty incumbent not on the child but on the parent.

Choosing the Participants

If you belong to a synagogue, the proper person to officiate at any life-cycle event is your rabbi. In larger congregations the *ḥazzan* (cantor) often performs many of these duties. If you live in a Jewishly isolated community, or if your synagogue does not have the services of a full-time rabbi or cantor, any knowledgeable Jewish adult may perform the ceremony. Parents should take an active role in bringing their children into the covenant. Rabbis' manuals are published by all the streams in modern Judaism, and any Hebrew-literate Jewish adult, with some preparation, can learn to officiate at a naming ceremony. Normally the rabbi or cantor officiates because he or she is both the most knowledgeable Jew in the community *and* an official representative of the community that the infant is about to join. In the absence of rabbi or cantor, however, there is nothing wrong with having a layperson perform the ceremony, even the parent.

Every synagogue has its own local *minhagim* (customs). When naming ceremonies are conducted in the synagogue, most congregations limit the number of people who are to be called to the *bimah.* Naming ceremonies on Friday evenings in a temple normally include only the parents and sometimes the baby, although some permit the inclusion of godparents.

In congregations where the traditional number of *aliyot* are called to the Torah on a Saturday morning, there are more opportunities to honor family members. A minimum of seven people are given the honor of reciting the blessing over the Torah reading, and others are called to lift and dress the Torah. In congregations where this is not the practice, godparents and grandparents might be given the honor of opening or closing the ark at the appropriate moments, or lighting Shabbat candles or reciting a prayer of thanksgiving.

Home ceremonies have more latitude. People you wish to honor might have the role of holding the baby, carrying her into the room, or reciting one or more of the blessings, especially *Ha-Motzi* at the start of the festive meal.

Again the important thing to keep in mind is that the role of *kvaterim* (godparents) should be assigned thoughtfully, with full cognizance of the position.

Can a Boy Have a Naming Ceremony?

An important aspect of both the *brit milah* and the naming ceremony is the introduction of a new person into the community. Traditionally a boy is named at the *brit milah* ceremony on the eighth day of his life.

Each community has its own customs and standards as to what is the correct and appropriate thing to do when naming a baby. Some Reform, Conservative, and Reconstructionist congregations offer naming ceremonies for both boys and girls.

The Law Committee of the Rabbinical Assembly (the professional organization of Conservative rabbis) has strongly recommended that naming ceremonies for boys should not take place and that Conservative rabbis should not officiate at them. You need to check with your rabbi for the standards and customs of your community.

Special Traditions

Naming Certificate

Although some Orthodox *mohalim* do not issue a certificate of *brit milah*, majority practice in North America is that boys receive such a certificate. Girls receive a certificate at their naming or other celebration marking their entrance into the covenant. Each of the streams has printed, standard certificates, some of which are quite beautiful. Your synagogue office carries a stock of such items. Many Jewish bookstores also carry such supplies. (If you live in relative Jewish isolation, most stores are willing to conduct transactions by mail.)

The certificate contains a place for the baby's full English and Hebrew name. Don't lose the certificate! When your child begins religious school, you will need to know his or her Hebrew name. For *Bar/Bat Mitzvah*, Confirmation, and weddings (the *ketubah* or wedding contract requires the full Hebrew names of the bride and groom), the certificate your child receives as an infant will be the authoritative document. Keep it in a safe place.

Shalom Zakhor

It is customary in some communities to mark the first Shabbat of a male child's life with a special celebration. On that Friday night, after dinner, relatives and friends gather at the baby's home to congratulate the family.

Biblical passages and psalms are recited, and a *d'var Torah* might be given. A light meal is also served. In some places, lentils and chickpeas are traditional foods because of their round shape, symbolizing life's continuity.

Shalom zakhor literally means "greeting the male." In Arabic the event is known as *shasha*, or *blada*.

Since we now celebrate the birth of a female with the same joy as for a male, some hold this gathering in honor of their baby girls as well. The only thing that needs to be changed is the name of the event. It becomes *shalom nekevah*, "greeting the female," or *shalom bat*, "greeting the daughter."

An Old Custom: The Wimpel

In Western Europe an interesting custom arose. The linen wrap worn by the baby at his *brit milah* was made into an embroidered Torah binder. The special piece of fine linen that was selected for the baby's swaddling cloth was cut into stripes, six inches wide, and sewn together to form a long ribbon. On it, the mother would then embroider the baby's name, date of birth, astrological sign, and any wishes that she might have for her new baby, including wishes for a life of Torah, *mitzvot*, good deeds, and a good marriage.

After the baby's first birthday the finished wimpel was presented to the family's congregation, a small ceremony accompanying the presentation. After the conclusion of the Torah service, the child was carried to the *bimah*, where the rabbi would offer a blessing over him. Then the wimpel was publicly displayed and was used that day as the Torah binder.

Many synagogues kept these wimpels in their archives, where they served as an important part of the historical record of the congregation. Unfortunately, most of these wimpels were lost during World War II and no longer exist.

The following human story recently appeared in a local Jewish newspaper:

An older man, a survivor of the Holocaust, recently toured an exhibit of memorabilia from Germany. Among the Torah scrolls, *yads*, and personal artifacts was a selection of wimpels that had been rescued from a Nazi collection of Jewish relics. One of the pieces in that collection was the wimpel that had been made for him by his mother!

Wimpel.
Germany, 1771

This custom of wimpel making is enjoying a revival today, as more and more Jews seek to make old traditions meaningful once again. Making a wimpel for your new baby is one way to express your creativity in an authentic Jewish art form, as well as an opportunity to create a historic memento for your baby and for the Jewish community as a whole.

An Older Custom: Pidyon Ha-Ben

Judaism has ancient roots. Jews have kept various customs and traditions alive over the course of the millennia, and of all the rituals we maintain and observe, *pidyon ha-ben*, the act of redeeming a firstborn son, truly smacks of antiquity.

In ancient days it was commonly believed that the gods were entitled to the first fruits and vegetables of both field and womb. The first fruits at harvest time, firstborn animals, and firstborn humans were all ritually sacrificed to the gods.

Judaism left these primitive rites behind and instead substituted a new custom. Any firstborn male, the "first issue" of a woman's womb (known in Hebrew as *peter rehem*), was to be consecrated to God as a priest or as a religious representative in the local communities of the time. This practice didn't last long, however, for, as the story goes, God changed His mind after the golden calf episode at Mount Sinai. When God saw the firstborn males committing idolatry, He offered the priestly responsibilities to the Levites, who then became God's ritual helpers on earth. Since that time we have followed the custom of releasing the firstborn male child of his ancient obligation with the following ceremony.

A table is set with ḥallah and a *kiddush* cup. The mother brings in the baby and hands him to the father, who is facing a Kohen, a Jew who traces his ancestry to the priestly class. The father has obtained five pieces of silver (silver dollars are often used) and has a dialogue with the *Kohen.*

The *Kohen* asks the father if he wishes to surrender his son for priestly service or if he wishes to ransom him for five pieces of silver. The father replies that he prefers to keep his son. (No other answer is acceptable.) He then recites two blessings and gives the *Kohen* the silver coins. Then the *Kohen* recites, "Your son is redeemed. Your son is redeemed. Your son is redeemed." A blessing is said over the ḥallah and wine and a festive meal is served to the invited guests. The ceremony is known as *pidyon ha-ben,* literally "the redemption of the son."

This ceremony may take place any time after the thirtieth day of life, whether there has been a *brit milah* or not. (Sometimes a *brit* is postponed because of ill health of the baby.) Thirty days is the age at which a baby is considered to be halakhically viable. *Pidyon ha-ben* may not take place on Shabbat or holidays when there are prohibitions against spending money.

Engraved depiction of Redemption of the First Born.

Holland, eighteenth century

This ritual need be performed only if the child is male and the first "issue" of the womb, and if the father is not a *Kohen* or a *Levite.* The rules also exclude babies born of cesarean section (for the baby is not considered to have "issued forth") and babies born after a previous miscarriage. Each woman can have only one firstborn, not one per husband, and if the firstborn is a girl, the law tells us that the ceremony does not take place.

Today, as we accord similar honors to male and female children, some parents like to celebrate the ritual for girls as well. A *pidyon ha-bat* (redemption of the daughter ceremony), though a departure from the traditional *halakhah,* can be seen as a warm expression of gratitude. In this case, no money need actually be exchanged, although a symbolic gift of *tzedakah* in the child's name would certainly be appropriate.

Can a Baby Convert to Judaism?

Usually conversion to Judaism requires consent, but in the case of small children, the Rabbis made an exception. They ruled that the parents are allowed to make the decision for the child, reasoning that conversion is an act that is done for the child's benefit. It can, therefore, be performed early in life. Later, if the child wishes to renounce Jewish status, that can be done at the age of majority. (Some consider "majority" to be the age of *Bar/Bat Mitzvah*, when Jewish children are expected to take on the responsibilities of our faith.)

The answer to the question of who is and who is not a Jew varies, depending upon whom you ask. In Orthodox and Conservative circles a baby must be born of a Jewish mother. In Reform and Reconstructionist circles a child may be considered a Jew if one parent (it doesn't matter which) is a Jew and if the child is being raised exclusively as a Jew. If the parents wish the child to be recognized unambiguously as Jewish by all members of the community, they can easily accomplish this through ritual conversion early in the child's life.

For a male, conversion can be partially accomplished at the *brit milah* on the eighth day of the child's life. The *mohel* or rabbi adds the appropriate prayers and blessings for the conversion during the *brit* ceremony. The conversion is not complete, however, until the baby is taken to the *mikveh* (ritual bath), and therefore the child's Hebrew name is not formally bestowed upon him during the *brit* ceremony. A *mikveh* is a warm pool, a portion of which must be rainwater, and it is built in a ritually prescribed manner. A parent enters the *mikveh* holding the baby and participates in the entire event with the child. The baby is fully immersed in the water for a moment, in the same manner as might be done at an infant swim class. After the immersion in the *mikveh*, the child receives his Hebrew name, and is considered to be halakhically Jewish by all standards. Usually a certificate attesting to the child's new status is issued at that time.

It is necessary for the circumcision to heal before the baby can be fully immersed in water. This fact separates the *brit milah* and the ritual immersion by a short period of time. The amount of time should be determined by your doctor or *mohel*.

If a non-Jewish boy who was circumcised medically at birth later wishes to become Jewish, a ceremony called *"hatafat dam brit"* is performed in conjunction with *mikveh;* one drop of blood is ritually and painlessly drawn from the gland of the penis. Some Reform and Reconstructionist rabbis do not insist upon this procedure.

Girls are also taken to the *mikveh* for ritual immersion and may then receive their Hebrew names. After this event, a naming ceremony may be performed for public recognition of the child's entrance into the covenant. Girls also receive a special certificate attesting to their new status.

For further information concerning conversion, *mikveh*, and the nature of the procedure, consult your rabbi.

Parents' Obligations to Their Children

Some people subscribe to a philosophy of parenting that sounds something like this: In order to raise happy and emotionally healthy children, you simply need to offer love and understanding. If you give them that, everything else will fall into place.

While it is true that love is a wonderful and important aspect of parenting, and that there is certainly no objection in Judaism to offering your child lots of love, our tradition does not stop there. The Talmud, with concern for the times when things might not always fall into place, expounds upon all aspects of financial and custodial responsibility. Such issues as divorce, custody, educational duties, and the age at which a child is no longer dependent are all discussed.

This talmudic excerpt is often quoted: A parent's obligations are "to circumcise him, to redeem him, to teach him Torah, to find him a wife, to teach him a trade," and some say, "to teach him to swim that he may save his life." If we look at this statement and all its implications with modern eyes, and then gender-neutralize it, it becomes a fairly complete list of our modern expectations as well.

Today, as then, we still bring our children into the covenant (with naming ceremonies and *brit milah*), we will spend great energy and expense on education, we still require that our children be trained in a profession from which they will gain both personal and financial reward, and we still attempt to teach our children to protect themselves from the hazards of life, whether that be by teaching them to swim or by some other means. We would still like to find our children appropriate spouses, though they don't often permit our doing so.

•••••••••••••••••◆•••••••••••••••

"Train up a child to know the proper path

to follow, and even when old,

the child will not depart from it."

•••••••••••◆•••••••••••

PROVERBS 22:6

Perhaps there is a stereotype of an overly doting Jewish parent who provides to excess. As with all stereotypes, there may be some truth to it. However, by offering our children more than just love, we follow the example of generations past, who did their utmost to provide their children with a secure and successful future.

The Role of Children in Jewish Tradition

There is an ancient midrash, as follows: When Moses was offered the Torah on Mount Sinai, God asked for collateral before giving something so precious. God asked Moses to approach the people for a proper symbol of the covenant. First the Jews offered their jewelry, but God countered that the Torah was more precious than jewels. Next Moses offered our great leaders as the sign, but God wouldn't accept this either, for God said that our leaders were already committed. Finally, after much thought, the Jewish people offered their children to God, promising to teach their children Torah throughout the generations. This, the most precious gift a human being can offer, was acceptable to God, and we have been diligently teaching our children Torah ever since (Song of Songs Rabbah).

During the recitation of the *Shema*, we repeat this same promise with the words, "You shall teach these words diligently unto your children." Our tradition has many vehicles with which we can accomplish this awesome task, only one of which is formal schooling. We teach by personal example, by observing the *mitzvot*, and by bringing Judaism and the Jewish holidays into our homes.

Almost every holiday has a special role for children to play, making children central to our celebrations. The Passover *seder*, for example, is designed as a learning experience for children. Complete with stories, symbols that can be eaten, active participation (e.g., opening the door for Elijah), and the specific role of the recitation of the Four Questions, Passover is a home holiday that invites the participation of children.

The same is true of Simḥat Torah, Purim, and Ḥanukkah. It is our children who create the noise and enthusiasm, who play the holiday games with a passion to win. Even at the Shabbat table, we take the time to bless each child individually.

The Torah portion known as the "Binding of Isaac" tells of God's demand that Abraham sacrifice his only son, Isaac. It ends, however, with the words, "and they rose up and went together to Beer-sheba." It is significant that after all the trials and tests to which God subjects Abraham and his son Isaac, they are able to walk on in life together, to remain forever bound by that invisible thread of faith. We too are inextricably bound to our children. They are our collateral, we are their teachers. We help them grow, and they, in return, keep us vital and strong.

On Becoming Bar/Bat Mitzvah

"If I am not for myself, who will be for me?

If I am only for myself, what am I?

And if not now, when!"

AVOT 1:14

A Link to the Past, A Bridge to the Future

When Moses stood on Mount Sinai, he asked why some of the Hebrew letters in the Torah were decorated with elaborate crowns. God replied, "In time a sage named Akiba will arise. Not only will he interpret the letter of the law, but the meaning contained in each of these decorative crowns." Moses asked to see this sage, and God said, "Turn around."

Moses turned and found himself among the students of Rabbi Akiba. Moses listened, but he could not understand the discussion. Nothing that Akiba taught seemed at all familiar to him. Moses was dispirited. Why had he, Moses, been chosen to receive the Torah when there would arise a teacher so much greater than he? Just then one of the students asked how the sage knew the meaning of a certain law, and Akiba replied, "This is the law as our master Moses taught it." So Moses became aware that, although each of us occupies a unique place in the chain of Jewish tradition, Judaism continues to grow and progress.

Like Judaism itself, the ceremony of Bar and Bat Mitzvah has developed over time. If Moses had been granted a vision of a modern Bat or Bar Mitzvah, he might not have recognized its significance, for the Torah ordains no ritual for the moment a child achieves the full privileges and responsibilities of a Jewish adult. Even Rabbi Akiba might not have understood its import, since no such ceremony existed in talmudic times.

Yet in our century Jews consider the Bar Mitzvah and Bat Mitzvah ceremonies the most salient reminders of the unique place of each Jew in the chain of tradition. For parents and teachers, the ceremony is a reminder of the role they play in transmitting Jewish heritage from one generation to the next. For the child, the ceremony marks the point at which Jewish study should result in Jewish action—the point at which he or she becomes a role model for Jewish children of generations to come.

Bar or Bat Mitzvah is a ritual, and as with all rituals, we must invest it with meaning. If we do not understand its underlying intentions, we may lose the value of the moment. Meaningful participation in this ceremony begins with knowing what is happening and why.

This chapter answers basic questions about the celebrations of Bar and Bat Mitzvah. Girls and boys can read it with their parents to share a sense of what will happen and why. Adults can find answers to questions about the ceremony— whether it is a ceremony planned for their children or one they intend for themselves. Those who are not Jewish but who are invited to a Bar or Bat Mitzvah can gain an understanding of what this ceremony means to the celebrants, to the family, to congregation members, and to the Jewish people as a whole.

Seymour Rossel

$\mathcal{G}$etting $\mathcal{R}$eady

Bar Mitzvah/Bat Mitzvah: A Call to Action

The words *Bat Mitzvah* and *Bar Mitzvah* are Hebrew terms indicating that a person has reached the status of an adult member of the Jewish community. The Bar Mitzvah and Bat Mitzvah ceremonies mark this transition from childhood to adulthood.

Bar Mitzvah is a masculine noun, and *Bat Mitzvah* is the same noun in feminine form. Both can be translated as "child of (God's) commandments." More precisely, becoming a Bat or Bar Mitzvah means accepting a transition: as a Jew becomes an adult, he or she accepts God's commands as binding in much the same way as a child accepts the commands of parents. We often hear Jews using these terms as verbs, speaking of being "Bar Mitzvahed" and "Bat Mitzvahed," and while this usage is grammatically incorrect, it is strikingly apt. Bar or Bat Mitzvah requires intense activity. A person may study Judaism and Hebrew for years in preparation for this ceremonial recognition. Families spend long hours planning the occasion to make it memorable. *Bar Mitzvah* and *Bat Mitzvah* can indeed be seen as terms of action.

Reading from the Torah is a privilege reserved for Jewish adults.

The nouns *Bat Mitzvah* and *Bar Mitzvah* suggest even more. The terms *bar* and *bat* denote membership in a group. The Hebrew word *mitzvah* is sometimes used to mean a "good deed," but here it is used in its technical sense, referring to the commandments found in the Torah—traditionally reckoned at 613. A *Bat Mitzvah*, then, is a woman who is "subject to the commandments," or, even better, "a woman of responsibility." Similarly, *Bar Mitzvah* is "a man of responsibility." The terms may be applied to every Jewish man from the age of thirteen and to every Jewish woman from the age of twelve, whether or not a ceremony takes place. It is at this age that one becomes a woman of duty or a man of duty, committed to the ideals of Judaism, and remaining one forever. The purpose of the ceremony is to mark this passage into Jewish adulthood, with all the privileges and responsibilities of that new status. The ceremony enables family and friends and the religious community as a whole to celebrate together the continuity of tradition and faith.

First Steps to Jewish Commitment

It is good to study and to learn, but Judaism is a religion of action. In Judaism, learning must lead to doing.

Jewish conduct is governed by commandments known as mitzvot *(singular,* mitzvah*). We express our values by performing specific acts, and their performance is an important part of our preparation for becoming Bar or Bat Mitzvah. Some suitable actions for young people to undertake are listed below.*

Step 1
Plant a tree in Israel.
AHAVAT ZION (Devotion to the Promised Land)

Step 2
Turn off the lights when you leave a room.
BAL TASHḤIT (Concern for the Environment)

Step 3
Bring a homework assignment to an ill classmate.
BIKKUR ḤOLIM (Visiting the Sick)

Step 4
Invite a friend for Friday night dinner.
HAKHNASAT ORḤIM (Welcoming Guests)

Step 5
Run an errand for an elderly neighbor.
HIDDUR P'NAY ZAKEN (Respecting the Aged)

Step 6
Take on a new chore at home.
KIBBUD AV VA-EM (Honoring Parents)

Step 7
Contribute canned goods to a food drive.
MA'AKHIL RE–EVIM (Feeding the Hungry)

Step 8
Donate clothing for Jewish immigrants in your community.
PIDYON SHEVUYIM (Redeeming the Captive)

Step 9
Settle an argument between friends.
RODEF SHALOM (Pursuing Peace)

Step 10
Take a Saturday afternoon stroll with your family.
SHABBAT (Honoring the Sabbath)

Step 11
Visit a Jewish museum or exhibit.
TALMUD TORAH (Increasing Knowledge)

Step 12
Get the ASPCA's list of cruelty-free products.
TZA'AR BA'ALEY ḤAYYIM (Being Kind to Animals)

Choosing the Right Time

The celebration marking a Bar or Bat Mitzvah usually takes place when the boy or girl reaches the age of thirteen. Traditionally, a girl became subject to the commandments at twelve years and a day, and a boy one year later. In common practice, however, the ceremony is usually observed either immediately before or after the youngster's thirteenth birthday. Some more traditional communities still retain the age difference set in ancient times, but the ceremony itself is a more recent tradition and can be celebrated at any time—even long after a person has achieved the status of majority.

The Mishnah (the oldest and postbiblical collection of Jewish laws) states that vows made by a boy who is thirteen years and one day old are considered valid and that he is eligible to lead the congregation in prayer, to serve on a Jewish court, and to buy and sell property. From the age of twelve, girls were eligible for all the obligations and privileges of Jewish women. It should be noted that many of the ritual obligations traditionally fell upon men, whereas women were not obligated to observe commandments that had to be carried out at fixed times. Jewish tradition has always respected the roles of both sexes, and today we are finding new ways to actualize that respect. The role of women within Judaism has greatly expanded, and—as strides toward achieving full equality continue—women now serve as rabbis and cantors within the Reform, Conservative, and Reconstructionist Movements.

Painting. A Boy's Bar Mitzvah. *France, ca. 1865 by E. Brandon*

The Rabbis considered a thirteen-year-old boy and a twelve-year-old girl to be physically and emotionally mature. They believed that, at these ages, girls and boys could tell right from wrong and could be held responsible for their own actions. Today, although we may consider thirteen as too young for people to be held responsible for *all* their decisions, we recognize the entry of youngsters into the teenage years as significant. As children reach their teens, they mature physically and intellectually and they begin to relate to the world in new ways. They begin to examine adult beliefs with varying degrees of skepticism. If a young person is properly prepared, the Bar or Bat Mitzvah ceremony can help him or her to reach independence via an impressive spiritual experience which speaks both to the intellect and to the soul.

"At five years the age is reached

for the study of Bible; at ten for the study

of Mishnah; at thirteen for the

fulfillment of the commandments. . ."

AVOT 5:21

The ceremony of Bar Mitzvah began in medieval times and was initially a minor ritual. The Bar Mitzvah boy was called to the Torah on a day soon after his thirteenth birthday. Since the Torah is read publicly during worship services on the Sabbath, on Monday, and on Thursday, any one of these days could be selected for a Bar Mitzvah. A simple meal served in the home enhanced the celebration. Because work was required in making and serving the meal, and because travel might be required, a Monday or Thursday was usually preferred out of respect for Shabbat observance. Following the worship service, the boy might also have delivered a short speech at his parents' home. Friends and relatives, especially the teachers and rabbis of the community, were invited.

The modern ceremony of Bat Mitzvah for girls is a product of twentieth-century American Jewry. On Friday evening, May 5, 1922, Rabbi Mordecai Kaplan, founder of the Reconstructionist Movement and a believer in the equality of the sexes, conducted the first Bat Mitzvah ceremony for his own daughter, Judith. The ceremony was soon adopted by the Reform Movement, it later was embraced by the Conservative Movement, and most recently the Orthodox Movement has also found ways of marking this rite of passage.

As Bat Mitzvah and Bar Mitzvah ceremonies became more important to American Jews, the Shabbat morning worship service became the preferred time to celebrate. Ceremonies can also be held on certain holidays or on the first day of a new month *(Rosh Ḥodesh)*, since the Torah is also read on these occasions.

The choice of the date may be affected by other considerations. A child whose birthday is in the summer may choose to wait until the fall to celebrate so that

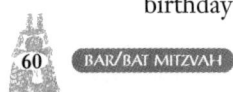

school friends can be present. In a large congregation, where two or more children may become eligible for Bar Mitzvah and Bat Mitzvah on the same date, they may celebrate together or one find another available date on the synagogue calendar. (The date is usually assigned a year or two before the ceremony takes place.) Sometimes parents schedule the celebration on a date when out-of-town relatives and friends can more easily make the trip. For families who choose to celebrate in Israel, the date may be dependent on travel arrangements. The date may occur before the English birthday, but it usually falls as soon after the Hebrew birth date as possible. Your rabbi can advise you.

"Precious is a command

fulfilled at its proper time."

SIFRA 25A

What has remained constant throughout the centuries is the custom of scheduling the ceremony on a day when the Torah is read. The reading of the Torah forms the core of the celebration, and Torah—Jewish learning—is its theme.

Preparation and Study

For more than two thousand years Jewish parents have had the responsibility of educating their children, raising them to become links in the chain of Jewish tradition. The best-known of all Jewish prayers, the *Shema*, contains a commandment to all Jewish parents: "You shall teach the commandments diligently to your children." The Rabbis of the Talmud maintained that the world was dependent on this education. In their words: "The world exists only through the breath of schoolchildren."

A Jewish legend says that God withheld giving the Torah to the Jewish people until they could provide some form of surety. When they finally pledged their children, God accepted this guarantee. Therefore, the legend concludes, each new generation must be taught the Torah and all that is in it, for the vitality of Torah depends upon its interpretation and transmission from generation to generation.

Thus Jewish schooling continues, although the structure of educational institutions has changed. Today Jewish children study Judaism either in supplementary schools, which specialize in the transmission of Jewish subjects, or in day schools, in which Jewish studies are integrated into the curriculum. In either case, Jewish parents must demonstrate their devotion to an ancient ideal in modern times.

Jewish tradition regards education as a lifelong concern leading to the ideal goal of study for its own sake. Bat Mitzvah and Bar Mitzvah are milestones in a lifetime of study. During four or five years of formal instruction, girls and boys acquire knowledge about Jewish customs and ceremonies, Jewish history, values, the Hebrew language, and Bible.

Hebrew reading is usually an important component of this training, and its mastery gives students great satisfaction. The study of Hebrew is valued among Jews

for several important reasons. The Torah and other books of the Bible are written in Hebrew. Jews throughout the world pray in Hebrew. Hebrew is the spoken language of the modern State of Israel. And it is the Hebrew language that unites Jews throughout the world in a shared culture. For all these reasons, a demonstration of the ability to read Hebrew is central to Bat Mitzvah and Bar Mitzvah ceremonies.

The formal presentation for Bar and Bat Mitzvah intensifies during the year preceding the special day. During the months and weeks leading to the ceremony, girls and boys study with the rabbi and the cantor of the congregation and often meet with a special instructor. Young people are intent on honing their skills for participation in the synagogue service. Their parents are also busy preparing for the celebration. All this important activity brings opportunities for a family to become more familiar with Jewish practice, to contemplate the ideas behind Jewish ritual, and to identify more strongly with the Jewish community.

The family may be invited to meetings or a retreat with other families whose children are preparing for their Bar or Bat Mitzvah celebrations. This is a good time to learn about the ceremony and the *mitzvot* associated with it. The candidate or the entire family may be encouraged to engage in some meaningful act of *tzedakah*, charity, on behalf of less fortunate people. This demonstration of how Jewish study leads to Jewish action adds a crucial dimension to the celebration. The family may be asked to attend synagogue services for a period of time preceding the ceremony. Attending services helps ensure familiarity with the customs of the particular congregation. All of these activities will help to prepare the celebrant and the family for the spiritual significance of this important rite of passage.

Every family is unique. Where families are "blends" of two earlier families or where there are family members of different faiths, special sensitivities are in order. Judicious adjustments in the ceremony may be required. Some synagogues have special arrangements for involving relatives who are not Jewish. In all cases, the rabbi and cantor of a congregation should be consulted and the policies of the synagogue respected. And certainly, in all families the emotional needs and sensitivities of all parties concerned should be carefully considered. Above all, the child's personal sense of privilege and responsibility are paramount.

 The Setting

The Synagogue and Its Symbols

Bat and Bar Mitzvah ceremonies usually take place in the synagogue. The drama of the celebration is heightened by the presence of the Torah scroll and other religious symbols. Many of the ritual objects seen in Jewish sanctuaries date back to the beginnings of Judaism. They are intended to remind worshippers of basic beliefs, values, and a shared history. Here are some basic facts about sanctuary objects and their meaning.

The Holy Ark, or *Aron Ha-Kodesh*, dominates one wall of a synagogue. Covered by a curtain or doors or both, it contains one or more Torah scrolls. This arrange-

ment reminds us of the Ark containing the tablets of the Ten Commandments which was carried by the Israelites during their years of wandering in the wilderness. The *Aron Ha-Kodesh* is usually on a raised platform *(bimah)*, which often has a speaker's podium. It is placed on the eastern wall so that as congregants face it they look toward Jerusalem.

The Torah scroll *(Sefer Torah)* stored in the Holy Ark contains the Five Books of Moses, the first five books of the Bible. The Torah is written on parchment made from animal skin, usually sheepskin. No vowels appear in the Torah scroll, because the vowel system as we now know it was introduced to the Hebrew language many years after the first scroll was written. The parchment is attached to two wooden rollers—each of which is called a Tree of Life *(Etz Ḥayyim)*—and clothed in a mantle of embroidered fabric.

Silver ornaments may adorn the top of the handles, or a crown may be used to cover them. A silver breastplate is placed at the front of the scroll. Also a carved silver *yad*, or "hand," is attached; the reader uses this *yad* to follow the text.

Above the Ark, the Eternal Light or *Ner Tamid* burns continuously. Often there is a representation of the tablets of the Ten Commandments and a seven-branched candelabrum, a *menorah*.

These familiar symbols transform the ordinary world into a sacred one in which prayer is natural and appropriate. Judaism helps us to create spiritual feelings within ourselves by creating a holy place—a house of God.

Traditional Attire

Bar and Bat Mitzvah ceremonies involve all the elements of liturgical drama. The words and actions are carefully prepared and the music is thoughtfully planned. But these ceremonies should not be seen as "theatrical" performances. Rather they are religious moments shared with God—moments designed to enhance spiritual goals. Those seated in the synagogue are not an "audience" but a community of faith gathered in congregation.

Careful attention is paid to two items of traditional attire: a skullcap, or *kippah*, and a prayer shawl, or *tallit*. They are worn by most Bar Mitzvah boys, and many Bat Mitzvah girls also wear them. While their use is optional in Reform practice, it is mandatory for men in Conservative and Orthodox synagogues. In fact, many Orthodox Jews keep their heads covered at all times.

The *kippah* is often referred to by its Yiddish name, *yarmulke*. During the late Middle Ages the practice of covering the head for prayer and study became universally accepted among Jews. In the nineteenth century the Reform Movement chose to leave heads uncovered in prayer, since con-temporary society viewed the removal of head coverings as a sign of respect. Recently, how-ever, more and more male Reform Jews have been choosing to wear the *kippah*. All Orthodox and many Conservative women wear a hat, a scarf, or a small lace kerchief on their head in the synagogue.

Embroidered silk *kippah*.
Poland, nineteenth century

Some women wear a *kippah*. During the Bar and Bat Mitzvah ceremony, the cele-brants and their families generally follow the custom of their congregation.

The *tallit* is a four-cornered garment which is draped around the shoulders. At each corner are knotted fringes called *tzitzit*. Their purpose is explained in the Torah: *God spoke to Moses saying: Speak to the children of Israel and enjoin them to make for themselves* tzitzit *on the corners of their garments throughout the generations. . . . Thus shall you be reminded to observe all My Commandments and be holy to your God.* (Numbers 15:37–40)

The *tallit* may be large or small, of any color, and made of any material, although wool and linen are never used together. (This mixture is forbidden in Deuteronomy 22:11.) The *tallit* has to meet only two requirements: it must have four corners, and each corner must have a white knotted fringe made of wool or of the same material as the *tallit*. Since the Torah commands that we be able to "see" the *tzitzit*, it is worn only in the daytime, although those who lead the prayer ser-vice may wear one in the evening. Once a year, on Yom Kippur, the *tallit* is worn in the evening as well. On this holiest day of the Jewish year, the prayers formally begin in the late afternoon before sunset, and so the *tallit* can remain on for the extended services, giving this service a special atmosphere of purity.

The wearing of a *tallit* is a privilege and mark of adulthood, serving as a constant reminder of the commandments. A boy officially wears a *tallit* for the first time on the occasion of becoming a Bar Mitzvah. Where it is used by women, a girl officially dons this robe of honor for the first time at the Bat Mitzvah ceremony as well.

Tefillin

Tefillin consist of two black leather boxes attached to knotted leather straps. The use of *tefillin* is explained in the Torah: "You shall bind them [God's words] as a sign upon your hand, and they shall serve as symbols before your eyes" (Exodus 13:9, 13:16; Deuteronomy 6:8, 11:18). Each leather cube is known by the part of the body to which it is attached. One is called "(of the) hand," *shel yad*, the other is called "(of the) head," *shel rosh*. Each cube contains specific passages from the Torah (Deuteronomy 6:4–9; 11:13–21; Exodus 13:1–10, 11–16). The passages in each cube are the same, but their arrangement is different.

Tallit with embroidered initials.

Russia, nineteenth century

Tefillin are not widely used in the Reform Movement, but Orthodox and Conservative Jews continue to wear them during weekday services. They are never worn on Shabbat or other Jewish holidays, because the holidays already are signs of the covenant. For this reason, they are seldom in evidence at the Bat Mitzvah or Bar Mitzvah ceremony, although sometimes boys and girls practice putting them on as part of their formal training.

The Ceremony

The Order of the Prayer Service

A rabbi was once asked by his students, "What do you do before praying?" He answered, "I pray that I may be able to pray properly." For most of us, praying with devotion is a challenge. To help us, the morning Jewish prayer service begins with meditations, songs, and blessings designed to create the proper mood in the mind of the worshipper. The length of this introduction may vary from congregation to congregation.

The main portion of the service begins with a two-sentence "Call to Prayer," the *Barekhu* (translated as *Bless Adonai, Who is to be blessed!*). In ancient times the priests would sing this prayer over the walls of the Temple to call the people from the marketplace. Modern Jews recite this same call at the beginning of the service.

The section that follows is called the *"Shema and its Blessings."* This portion of the prayer service emphasizes God's relationship to Israel. There are two prayers before the *Shema* and one after it. The first prayer praises God as the creator of all things. The second prayer speaks of the covenant between God and the Jewish people. The *Shema* itself contains biblical passages which tell what we must do to be a part of the Jewish covenant and what God promises in return. Finally, the prayer after the *Shema* acknowledges God's role as the redeemer of Israel.

The next section of the service has several names. It is sometimes called the *Shmoneh Esray*, the "Eighteen Benedictions" (although there are actually nineteen today). It may also be called the *Amidah*, the "Standing Prayer," since the prayer is said while standing. Most commonly, however, it is known as the *Tefillah*, "the Prayer," because it serves as the central prayer of the service. The blessings in the *Tefillah* vary from one service to another, but their essential ingredient is the statement of the needs of the Jewish community and personal petitions. On Shabbat we are encouraged to appreciate what we already have, so the petitionary blessings are replaced by one that thanks God for the gift of the Sabbath, leaving only six other blessings on that day.

On days when we read publicly from the Torah scroll, a special Torah service is inserted at this point for removing the Torah from the Holy Ark, reading it, hearing the *haftarah* portion (the reading from the Prophets on Shabbat and the festivals), and then replacing the scroll in the Ark. Blessings are recited before and after the reading of both the Torah and the *haftarah*. On Sabbath and Holy Days, the Torah service may be followed by the *Musaf*, or "Additional" service.

The service concludes with several prayers and a closing hymn. One of these is the *Alenu*, a prayer for the perfection of the world. Another closing prayer is the "Mourner's Prayer," the Mourner's *Kaddish*. This prayer was originally said only for sages who had died; today it is recited by a mourner following the passing of a close relative and on the anniversary of the death. Remarkably, this prayer does not speak of death at all but rather praises God and asks for the speedy coming of the age of peace.

This is a simplified outline of a Jewish prayer service. Looking at the construction of the service, we perceive it moving in an intentional direction: We prepare to pray, we hear the call to formal prayer, we reflect on our loving relationship with God, and—standing within that relationship—we petition for our communal and personal needs. We are drawn closer to God through our sacred texts, and then restored to ourselves. When we return to ourselves, we are to be changed. As it is said, "Those who rise from prayer better persons, their prayer is answered."

Aliyah: *Being Called to the Torah*

It is always an honor to be called up to recite the blessings before and after the Torah scroll is read. This act is known as an *aliyah*, literally, "ascending." It takes its name from the fact that the worshipper ascends the *bimah*, the platform, but this physical act of going up is symbolic of a greater spiritual one. The act of moving from the Diaspora to the Land of Israel is also called *aliyah*. And for those who are

in Israel, all travel in the direction of Jerusalem or the Temple mount is "ascending," while all travel away from Jerusalem is referred to as "descending." The synagogue worshipper called to the Torah makes a symbolic spiritual ascent.

On the day of a young person's first *aliyah*, family and friends have the opportunity to share the honor. On the Sabbath, the Torah portion is traditionally divided into at least seven sections. (Sometimes additional divisions are added.) In the talmudic period each person who was called for an *aliyah* read the Torah portion, but today the reading is generally done by a trained individual. The person who is honored with an *aliyah* recites a blessing before the reading and another after it. In some congregations an *aliyah* can be shared, with individuals reading together.

There are many occasions on which a Jewish adult may be honored with an *aliyah*. An engagement, the birth of a child, recovery from a serious illness, a daughter's Bat Mitzvah, a son's Bar Mitzvah, a wedding anniversary, a *yahrzeit* commemorating the death of a relative—all these and more may be reasons for begin honored in this way. The one most pertinent to our discussion is the special honor reserved for one who is called to the Torah for the first time.

Traditionally, the Bar Mitzvah is called for the recitation of the final portion of the Torah reading. In synagogues where women perform the same religious roles as men, the Bat Mitzvah is also called for this final portion. The person who receives the honor of reciting this portion is referred to as the *maftir* (for a male) or *maftirah* (female), the one who "concludes." All are usually called to the *bimah* by their Hebrew names.

Reciting the Torah blessings is symbolic of the young person's acceptance of adult Jewish responsibilities. The young person is now making the journey upward officially for the first time—the first *aliyah*—an act that echoes the very first *aliyah*, when Moses ascended Mount Sinai to receive the Torah. This connection transforms all the arduous preparation into a sacred religious act as the youngster becomes a full participating member of the Jewish community, committed to its historic covenant with God.

As part of the service, the Bar Mitzvah and Bat Mitzvah also generally read from the Prophets. A prophetic selection from this part of the Bible has been assigned to each Torah portion, and this is read at the conclusion of the Torah service. This sec-

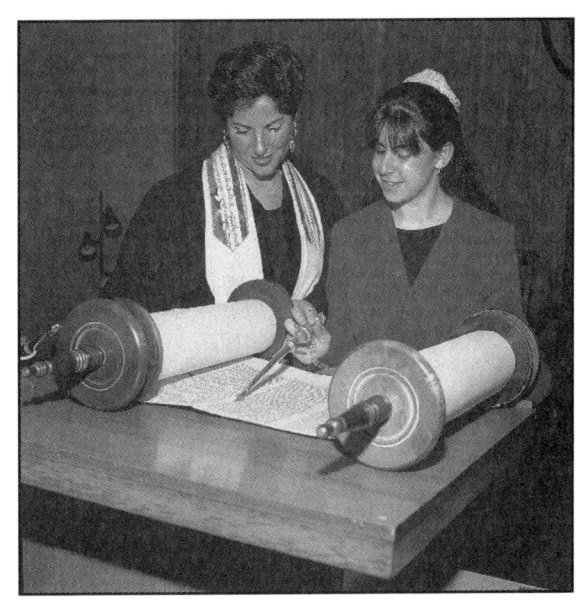

A carved yad or "hand" is used when one is reading the Torah so that the natural oils of the hand will not smear the ink.

tion is called the *haftarah*, the "conclusion." Each selected reading is related in some way to the ideas in the specific Torah portion or to the time of the year.

Special blessings are recited before and after the *haftarah* is read. The blessing before the reading stresses the divine inspiration of the prophets. After the *haftarah* reading, the reader thanks God for giving the Torah, Shabbat, Israel, and the prophets, and for the opportunity to worship.

In some synagogues the girl or boy may recite only the blessings and a few verses of the prophetic portion, while in others the entire *haftarah* is recited. In all cases, the *haftarah* reading is central to Saturday morning Bar or Bat Mitzvah ceremonies.

Chanting with Trop

It is sufficient simply to read aloud the Torah and *haftarah* portions. However, there are special melodies traditionally assigned to this part of the service. These melodic chants, which are part of ancient tradition, are indicated by means of printed notations which students may learn. Several terms have been used for these melodies, but the most common is *trop*.

The earliest known book containing musical notation for the Torah *trop*.

Johannes Reuchli. Germany, 1518

The purpose of chanting Torah with *trop* is to organize the text. In earlier times punctuation marks were uncommon (the Torah portion is still read from an unmarked scroll). *Trop* gives shape to the text by separating thoughts and properly accenting words and phrases. Most people believe that in the Middle Ages these signs were indicated by a use of hand and finger motions between the teacher and the student. The relationship of the particular melody to the text is sometimes arbitrary, but a well-educated student can find associations between the words and the melody. In addition, the melodies are quite beautiful in their own right. There are special chants used on the High Holy Days and for reading the scrolls of Ruth, Esther, Ecclesiastes, Lamentations, and Song of Songs at the appropriate festival times, and there is even a chant for the study of Mishnah.

In the ancient world, sacred texts were always chanted. The melodies evoke a deeper commitment to our sacred texts when we understand that this musical tradition is very much a part of classic Jewish ritual.

Derashah: *A Special Message*

The tradition of having the celebrant deliver a short speech is not a new one. This speech, which is called a *derashah*, is often based on an aspect of the assigned Torah or *haftarah* portion. Originally learned members of the community, along with family and a few friends, gathered together on the afternoon of the Bar Mitzvah day to hear the *derashah*. Today, however, the speech is generally woven into the Bat or Bar Mitzvah ceremony in the synagogue. Rabbis, teachers, and parents may help the young person with the speech. In some congregations the speech is divided into

three parts: a commentary on the Torah portion, a commentary on the *haftarah*, and a discussion of the meaning of the ceremony.

The *derashah* provides an opportunity for the celebrant to express Jewish feelings. Yet its main purpose is to show that the Bar or Bat Mitzvah not only has mastered the skills necessary for the prayer service but also understands the Torah and *haftarah* readings for the day. Jewish texts can always be viewed from a new angle, from a broader perspective, incorporating personal experiences. The study of Judaism is often likened to the sea—no matter where one jumps in, the sea stretches out in all directions. And so we turn to the words of Torah again and again to understand their message more fully.

"I am a Jew because in every age when the

cry of despair is heard the Jew hopes.

I am a Jew because in all places where there

are tears and suffering the Jew weeps.

I am a Jew because the message of Israel is

the most ancient and the most modern."

"WHY I AM A JEW," EDMOND FLEG

A nineteenth-century German engraving by Moritz Oppenheim depicts the Bar Mitzvah delivering a *derushah* to family and guests.

The Role of Parents

Watching as one's child achieves adulthood by performing the ritual of Bat or Bar Mitzvah is cause for rejoicing. Jewish tradition sees a child's spiritual growth and moral development as great accomplishments. When a child has an understanding of ethical behavior, it is a pleasure to release that child into the world.

Beyond rejoicing, parental participation in the ceremony itself is limited. During talmudic times it was customary for a father to recite a brief blessing at having been freed from the responsibility for his son's observance of religious law. In modern Orthodoxy this tradition continues. In Reform, Conservative, and Reconstructionist synagogues parents often recite the *Sheheḥeyanu* blessing.

In Orthodox synagogues the father and male friends and relatives may be honored during the ceremony by being called to participate in the service, particularly the Torah service. In Reform, Conservative, and Reconstructionist congregations, where both men and women are included, the most common custom is to have the mother and father receive an *aliyah*. There may also be a ceremony in which the Torah scroll is passed from generation to generation: first to grandparents, who pass it to the child's parents, who pass it to the young person celebrating. This ritual symbolizes the unbroken chain of Jewish tradition. In some congregations the parents may personally address their son or daughter. In cases where not all family members are Jewish, sensitive treatment of these relatives enables everyone to feel comfortable. The officiating rabbi should, of course, be consulted about the congregation's custom regarding the participation of relatives.

Children with Special Needs

Every individual in the world is unique. Since no person is exactly like another, the word "normal" as it is often applied to people has little significance. Each of us has unique abilities and unique disabilities, yet Jewish tradition teaches that all of us are created in God's image.

The Jewish child who is bound to a wheelchair, the one on crutches, the one who has vision only within, the one who must imagine the sounds of the outside world, the one whose words fall short of his or her intellectual abilities, the one who suffers diseases that others could not tolerate, the one whose abilities outstrip her or his understanding—all are precious in the sight of God.

Since almost all of the elements of Bar and Bat Mitzvah ceremonies are the result of custom and not law, a great deal of latitude can be exercised to accommodate any special needs of a child. The emphasis should be on what the girl and boy *can* do rather than on what might be too difficult for them. Certainly the celebrant is the center of attention, but perhaps much more can be achieved. Children with special needs are often able to accomplish goals that astound family, friends, and the congregation.

Rabbis, educators, and social workers are generally aware of institutions, such as the Jewish Braille Institute and P'TACH (Parents for Torah for All Children), which have developed special programs for Bar and Bat Mitzvah. The national movements—Conservative, Orthodox, Reconstructionist, and Reform—have all devoted

time and effort to considering the place of the child with special needs in Jewish life. Also, local Jewish federations, boards of Jewish education, and other community organizations often employ consultants with experience in the field of special needs.

> "God has stamped every person with
>
> the die of the first human, yet not one of
>
> them is like another."

SANHEDRIN 4:5

A ceremony for a child with special needs often requires adjustments. For instance, while it is customary for the entire congregation to be present at the ceremony, a more intimate gathering might be more suitable. Sometimes only the service's core is emphasized, to the exclusion of other prayers. Perhaps all that is possible is the party itself. The rabbis have called prayer "the service of the heart." In the case of a child with special needs, the dictates of the heart are an offering to God.

Adult Bar/Bat Mitzvah Ceremonies

Many synagogues have instituted programs for adult Bar and Bat Mitzvah. Sometimes the ceremony is held for an individual; often, it is a group project—an entire class of adults celebrating together. In either case, people who have experienced it report that it is one of life's most satisfying religious events.

In Judaism there is no one right time for study, because Jews see no time as wrong for it. While study may seem easier for the young, more mature students can draw on greater experience and can understand things more deeply. According to tradition, the great Rabbi Akiba did not begin the study of Torah until he was forty years old!

The ceremony and the study that precedes it affirm a deep commitment to the values of Jewish life and an affirmation of Jewish identity. Adult preparation often requires activities such as synagogue attendance, participation in charitable works, and study of Jewish history, customs, holidays, and basic religious concepts. Some may feel uncomfortable about being in a classroom after so many years, but they should be assured that the learning environment in the synagogue is warm and supportive. Other adults contemplating Bat or Bar Mitzvah may fear the need to master Hebrew reading; most are amazed to learn how easy it can be.

Even if they have already celebrated as children, adults can reaffirm the celebration by reading the Torah and *haftarah* portions once again. While affirming one's Jewish identity and exploring one's religious philosophy are personal matters, sharing this affirmation with the congregation is precisely what Bar Mitzvah and Bat Mitzvah are all about.

The Celebration

How to Celebrate

Bar Mitzvah and Bat Mitzvah are cause for celebration, a "joyous occasion," a *simḥah*. We are not the only people who express gratitude and joy with food and drink. This custom is shared by many other cultures, but Judaism has made it a sacred undertaking. A little history will help give a clearer understanding of the importance of feasting and religious celebration.

After the Temple in Jerusalem was destroyed, the Rabbis transferred much of the Temple ritual to the synagogue and to the home. Each meal was considered a sacred event; the dining table was viewed as a substitute for the Temple altar on which ancient rituals had been performed. Just as holy bread or "shewbread" had been placed on a golden table in the Temple, the Jewish table always has bread on it. Just as the priests had ceremonially cleansed their hands before conducting a sacrifice, the Rabbis prescribed a ritual washing of hands before eating. Blessings were ordained to consecrate the meal.

A special meal was instituted for the day of the circumcision of an infant boy. Since this was the day on which the infant entered into the covenant of Israel, the meal was called a *seudat mitzvah*—a feast accompanying the performance of a *mitzvah*. By medieval times, many authorities had drawn a bond between the ceremonies of circumcision and Bar Mitzvah, not only because they serve as the beginning and end of Jewish childhood, but also because both are concerned with the covenant. In the case of circumcision, parents determine to raise their child as a Jew; in the case of Bat and Bar Mitzvah, boys and girls assume responsibility for themselves as Jews.

The Bar Mitzvah feast likely began as a small meal served to guests who gathered at the boy's home to hear the *derashah*, or speech. As time went by, this practice developed into the custom of providing refreshments to the entire congregation after the prayer service. This light meal is called a *kiddush*, taking its name from the blessing recited over wine on the Sabbath eve and morning. The *kiddush* grew into a party, and the party later was separated from the *kiddush*.

As Bat and Bar Mitzvah parties developed in America, they often tended toward excess. An old joke that Bar Mitzvah celebrations had too much "bar" and not enough *mitzvah* can serve as a warning. There have been other times and places when excess apparently interfered with the religious significance of the celebration. In Eastern Europe in the seventeenth century a Jewish community in Poland placed specific limits on the amount of jewelry that people could wear to a Bar Mitzvah party. And about the same time a Lithuanian rabbi cautioned his congregation against spending too much money on the meals and the decorations.

Even in the best of times there are trouble, suffering, and pain. We can view the Bat or Bar Mitzvah celebration as an opportunity to sensitize ourselves and to teach our children the importance of financial restraint and the value of sharing with those who are hungry and homeless. A contribution to charity based on a percentage of the cost of the party might be a good example.

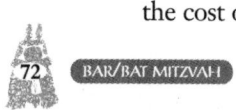

Among the sacrifices offered in the ancient Temple in Jerusalem was the grain sacrifice made in form of "shewbread." Dutch engraving of shewbread table, ca. 1700.

One whole area of Jewish values is devoted to which foods are "proper" and which are "improper." The term for this system is *kashrut*. The party should be seen as part of the *mitzvah*, and even the most liberal family should seek instruction on the Jewish dietary standards of the congregation.

Maintaining a degree of dignity is in keeping with the party's role as a *seudat mitzvah*, a meal celebrating the fulfillment of a commandment. When the celebration conveys a sense of warmth and caring for guests and active concern for others less fortunate in society, it then becomes a proper extension of the worship service that preceded it.

Enriching the Celebration with Meaningful Acts

The word *mitzvah* indicates that the Bar and Bat Mitzvah celebration is an opportunity to consider the needs of others and to perform acts to enhance the experience. Traditionally parents made a donation to the synagogue or the community in honor of the Bar Mitzvah of their son. In many communities the ultimate gift was the presentation of a Torah scroll. Short of this, adornments for the Torah, new prayer books, and ritual art were donated. Alternatively, contributions were made to underwrite funerals and weddings for the poor, or to help any of a thousand good causes sponsored by the Jewish community. These charitable practices continue today and are encouraged for families celebrating Bat Mitzvah and Bar Mitzvah.

In the search for deeper meaning, American Jews instituted the custom of "twinning." The family obtains the name of a thirteen-year-old Jew trapped in Ethiopia or Russia and includes this child's name on the invitation, stating in essence that the American celebrant will be called to the Torah on behalf of this child as well. A portion of the monetary gifts received might be set aside to help free the family of the "twinned" child or to free Ethiopian or Russian Jewry in general. Although the recent rescue of Ethiopian Jewry and the breakdown of the Soviet system may have made "twinning" on behalf of these two populations less meaningful, there remain Jews trapped in various ways. Today the girl or boy may be "twinned" with a poor child living in the United States or in the State of Israel, and contributions may be made to organizations working on behalf of the poor. Similarly, several Jewish communities remain trapped in Arab counties, and "twinning" with their children is still appropriate. Just as "twinning" was a response to a particular moment in time, other needs may arise which sensitive families may use as the springboards to new and creative ways to make Bar and Bat Mitzvah more meaningful.

·················◆·················

"Is study greater, or doing?"

Rabbi Tarfon said, "Doing is greater."

Akiba said, "Study is greater."

They concluded that study was greater,

for it led to doing.

·················◆·············

KIDDUSHIN 40B

Witnessing impoverished and hungry people in nearly every part of America, many young people choose to tithe, that is, to allot a portion of the monetary gifts they receive to a particular charity. The giving of *tzedakah* is a vitally important Jewish act. Some families forgo a large party, choosing instead to contribute to charity the money they might have spent or a special volunteer project can be planned, one that includes other family members and friends as well. For example, canned goods can replace traditional floral centerpieces and then be donated to a local shelter or food kitchen, and arrangements can be made for donating leftover food as well. Books, inscribed with guests' names, can be presented to the synagogue library. Selecting the appropriate charity and making the donation can express the word *mitzvah* in its highest sense.

Some families travel to Israel and hold the Bat or Bar Mitzvah ceremony there. Others hold the ceremony in their own synagogues and later enjoy an additional family experience in Israel. Many alternatives for the trip are possible; there are agencies and institutions that can help with the arrangements. There are many suitable locations in Israel, and for those with relatives living there, this trip can be particularly meaningful. Be sure to consult your rabbi.

The search for Jewish values need not lead a family far afield. There is no end to the ways in which people can reach out to help one another. All of these activities—whether easing the pain of human suffering or working to repair the world or striving to save animals on the brink of extinction—can add a significant dimension to the celebration and enhance the experience for the entire family.

The Importance of B'nai Mitzvah Ceremonies

The Jewish people have shown a remarkable aptitude for adaptation to changing times. This has been a mark of our creativity. At the same time, we are a tradition that embraces the past.

In talmudic times it was considered a sign of respect for men to bare the head, but by the middle of the seventeenth century the custom of covering the head as a

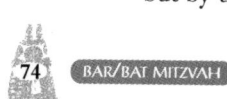

sign of submission to God's kingdom had become nearly universal. In ancient times the holiday of Sukkot was considered the most important one of the Jewish year, but when Jews were forced to leave the land of Israel, although the celebration of Sukkot continued, the holidays of Rosh Hashanah and Yom Kippur became more important. They were transformed into the High Holy Days. In ancient times three symbols were commonly used to identify Jewish buildings—the *lulav*, the *etrog*, and the incense shovel. Today the six-pointed "Star of David" has become a more significant marker. These are only a few examples of changes.

A change in emphasis reflects a change in cultural conditions. Bar Mitzvah and Bat Mitzvah are Jewish rituals that have great importance for us today, but they are not ordained in the Torah or mentioned in the Bible. Even in the Talmud, the term appears only as a designation for the ages of legal majority. Yet Bat Mitzvah and Bar Mitzvah have become integral to Jewish life.

Why do Bar and Bat Mitzvah continue to exercise such influence on us today? The answer grows out of the condition of our souls. In a time when faith is questioned on every side, there is an urgency to a Jew's affirming a commitment to the covenant that binds the Jewish people to God and God to us. In a time when rites of passage may be disparaged as primitive, there is a yearning for a milestone event to separate the early years of childhood from the years of adolescence and adulthood. In a time when mobility has spread families out across America—even dispersed them to the four corners of the earth—there is a need for a ceremony to bring families together with shared traditions. In a time when we seek the meaning of our Jewish identity, the Bat Mitzvah and Bar Mitzvah provide challenges and opportunities for creating meaning in our lives.

Bat and Bar Mitzvah observance helps to ensure the continuation of Jewish learning. It marks the acquisition of Jewish skills. It is the moment when the Jewish community grows by one member, then one more member, and then still one more. It strengthens the continuing vitality of Jewish life. It is a time that draws Jewish leaders closer to the people they serve. It trains children to achieve what is expected of adults, so it prepares them to be adults. It sets Jewish children on a life-long path toward wisdom, faith, justice, and peace.

Looking Ahead: Confirmation

Students who have achieved the goal of Bar or Bat Mitzvah are encouraged to continue their formal study of Judaism. Confirmation is an opportunity to do this.

In the nineteenth century the Reform Movement introduced Confirmation as a replacement for Bar Mitzvah. Since modern children lingered longer than in the past in their secular schooling and in their parents' homes, early Reform leaders argued that it was appropriate that they should not "graduate" too early from their Jewish schooling. While this argument had some logic, it flew in the face of the even more powerful tradition of Bar Mitzvah. In the 1940s the Bar Mitzvah ceremony was gradually restored to the Reform Movement. Reform Jewish thinkers came to view Bar and Bat Mitzvah as a time for an individual to make a personal commitment to Jewish identity, while Confirmation was seen as a time for a class of students to make a commitment to their Jewish identity as a group.

Many Conservative synagogues use Hebrew school graduation exercises in a similar fashion. Graduation from a Jewish day school also serves as a moment of affirmation for the graduating class.

Jewish education should be a lifelong process. As we grow and mature, our understanding deepens. When we truly understand the meaning of the term Bat Mitzvah—to be a "woman of responsibility"—and Bar Mitzvah—to be a "man of responsibility"—then this commitment to the Jewish people should be demonstrated by continued learning.

On the Death of a Loved One

"Our days are like grass;

we bloom like the flower of the field;

a wind passes by and it is no more."

PSALM 103:15–16

Tradition and Grief

Judaism embraces all of life and accepts death as a part of life. At the same time, Jewish tradition understands that we are never prepared to lose someone we love. In the face of death we are confronted by powerful emotions and questions to which we have no answers. That is when ritual shows its greatest strength. Judaism presents us with a highly structured series of procedures that can help us through our grief and ease us back into the rhythm of life. Jewish tradition recognizes our confused emotions and shows us how to act on them in clearly demarcated stages of mourning.

There is comfort and security in the knowledge that centuries of tradition lie behind each of these practices, as we do what our parents did before us and their parents before them.

Rabbi William Cutter

Preparing for a Funeral

What Is an Onen?

Upon the death of a loved one, until the time of burial, each immediate relative (parent, spouse, child, or sibling) is referred to as an *onen* (fem. *onenet*). Although in a state of shock and distress, the *onen* is occupied with the immediacy of practical arrangements. Some of these arrangements will require the advice and aid of your rabbi, the funeral home, and even hospital personnel.

Family and friends must be notified of the death. The *onen* usually does not receive condolence calls at this early stage; the family of the deceased is allowed the privacy of grief. Close friends, however, may offer to help with the funeral arrangements.

Because the *mitzvah* of caring for the dead is so important, the *onen* is freed of certain ritual obligations. For example, the *onen* need not pray, recite blessings, or put on *tefillin*. On Shabbat, however, many of the laws that pertain to the *onen* fall away. Shabbat observances are performed and synagogue services attended. Your rabbi should be consulted for more detailed information.

When the Funeral Takes Place

The funeral and burial are held as soon after death as possible. Judaism considers it a dishonor to the deceased to delay burial unnecessarily. In addition, prolonging the burial subjects the bereaved to even greater strain and despair. Usually the funeral is held early in the day. The exact timing, of course, depends on the availability of the funeral home and the schedule of the rabbi, who should be contacted before the time is set.

In certain circumstances the funeral can be delayed. Funerals are not held at the following time: on Shabbat; on the festival days of Passover, Shavuot, and Sukkot; or

Carrying the Body from the House.   *Prague, ca. 1780.*

on the High Holy Days. In special circumstances or when family and friends have to travel great distances to attend a funeral, a postponement is certainly acceptable.

Choosing a Casket

Judaism discourages ostentatious funerals. Loved ones are buried with simplicity and dignity. The traditional Jewish coffin is made of plain wood. It need not be lined or padded. Small holes are sometimes drilled in the bottom. The coffin may have metal handles or nails, although it is customary among traditional Jews to use wooden-pegged caskets. Sometimes a bag filled with earth from Israel is placed under the head, and some of the soil is sprinkled over the body. Usually no worldly possessions are placed in the coffin with the deceased, although the bereaved sometimes choose to put a small token of love into the casket.

Simplicity is always to be encouraged. In Israel, for example, the deceased is wrapped only in linens and is buried directly in the ground. Bodily remains are returned to the earth as quickly as possible

> "For dust you are and to dust
>
> you shall return"

GENESIS 3:19.

All branches of Judaism discourage the viewing of the body other than for proper identification. We are encouraged to remember our beloved ones in the vibrancy of their lives.

Before the body is buried, it is washed in a ritual act of purification called *taharah*. Just as a baby is washed and enters the world clean and pure, so do we leave the world cleansed by the religious act of *taharah*.

Making the Coffin. *Prague, ca. 1780.*

The cleansing is performed by the funeral director and staff, or the ritual of *taharah* may be carried out by the Ḥevrah Kaddisha ("holy society"). The Ḥevrah Kaddisha is a group of specially trained Jews who care for the body and prepare it for burial. They follow strict procedures, including the recitation of prayers and psalms. Men handle male bodies and women prepare female bodies; modesty is preserved even in death. You may consult your rabbi to find out if there is a Ḥevrah Kaddisha in your area.

In traditional Jewish practice the deceased is not left alone from the time of death until burial. This ritual act of *shemirah* ("watching," "guarding") is performed as a sign of respect to the deceased. A *shomer* ("watcher") may be hired to perform this service.

After the body is cleansed, it is dressed in shrouds (in Hebrew, *takhrikhim*). The shrouds are simple and plain and made of white cotton or linen. Some people are buried in their typical daily dress. Men are buried with a *tallit* over the shroud or suit. Women are sometimes buried in a *tallit* if it was their practice to wear one when praying. One of the fringes of the *tallit* is cut to show that it will no longer be used.

Expressing Grief through Keriah

Keriah is a Hebrew word meaning "tearing." It refers to the act of tearing one's clothes or cutting a black ribbon worn on one's clothes. This rending is a striking expression of grief and anger at the loss of a loved one.

Keriah is an ancient tradition. When our Patriarch Jacob believed his son Joseph was dead, he tore his garments (Genesis 37:34). Likewise, in II Samuel 1:11 we are told that King David and all the men with him took hold of their clothes and rent them upon hearing of the death of Saul and Jonathan. Job too, in grieving for his children, stood up and rent his clothes (Job 1:20).

Keriah is performed by the child, parent, spouse, and sibling of the deceased. It is usually done at the funeral home before the funeral service begins. If a black ribbon is used, it is provided by the funeral director. *Keriah* is always performed standing.

The act of standing shows strength at a time of grief. A cut is made on the left side of the clothing for deceased parents—over the heart—and on the right side for all other relatives. Sometimes people choose to express deep feelings of grief by cutting on the left side for relatives other than their parents.

As the tear or cut is made, the family recites the following blessing:

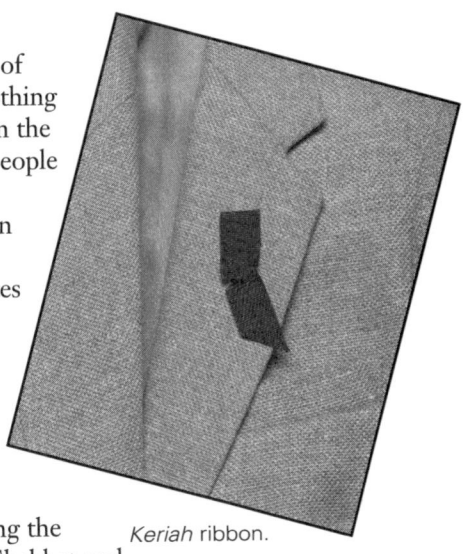

Keriah ribbon.

> *Barukh atah, Adonai Eloheinu,*
> *melekh ha-olam, dayan ha-emet.*
>
> Blessed are You, Adonai our God,
> Ruler of the world, Judge of Truth.

The torn garment or ribbon is worn during the seven days of *shiva* (see page 86), except on Shabbat and festival days. Some people continue the practice for the thirty-day period of mourning.

The Funeral and the Interment

The Funeral Service

Jewish funerals are characterized by brevity and simplicity. They are designed for the honor and dignity of the deceased and are a part of the mourning process which helps comfort the bereaved.

At one time the funeral service began in the home of the deceased. Psalms were recited, and a procession led the body to the burial site. Today the larger portion of the service takes place in the funeral chapel or synagogue. Sometimes the entire service is conducted at the gravesite.

The bereaved family is seated in the front row of the chapel or synagogue. The closed coffin remains in view. Traditionally the coffin is not decorated with flowers. Instead of sending flowers in the name of the deceased, a donation can be made to charity.

A brief introductory piece of music is sometimes played. This music is usually selected from the Jewish tradition and should be simple and not overly sentimental.

The service may begin with one or more psalms. The one most commonly recited is Psalm 23. The rabbi, cantor, or leader of the service then proceeds with several readings from Psalms or other inspirational sources.

The eulogy is most often delivered by the rabbi, who has met with the family prior to the funeral to learn about the deceased and the particular attributes the family would like mentioned. The eulogy typically contains personal reminiscences and sometimes humorous anecdotes as well. Often the family will write down special memories they have of the deceased which the rabbi then reads. The

The Eulogy. *Prague, ca. 1780.*

process of writing can help the family; they are comforted when their own words are read. The eulogy may also be delivered by a member of the family or a close friend.

The final prayer of the funeral service is the memorial prayer *El Malei Raḥamim* (Hebrew for "God, full of compassion"):

> *Exalted God full of compassion, grant the fullness of Your peace to the soul of _____, who has gone to his (her) eternal rest. May (s)he share in the glory of the upright, the luster of whose purity is as the brightness of the firmament. His (Her) memory lives in the hearts of his (her) dear ones as an inspiration to deeds of charity and goodness. May (s)he be granted the bliss of eternal life. Shelter him (her) forever, merciful God, under the wings of Your protecting love, and may his (her) soul be bound up in the bond of eternal life. God is his (her) possession. May (s)he rest in peace. Amen.*

At the close of the service an announcement is made informing those present where and when the initial seven-day period of mourning will be observed.

The Burial

At the conclusion of the chapel service, family along with those friends who wish to attend the burial service form a procession behind the hearse and travel in convoy to the gravesite. Accompanying the dead is a *mitzvah* in the Jewish tradition.

At the burial site the casket is removed from the hearse and carried by the pall-bearers to the grave. The rabbi leads the procession. Usually at least six people are needed to carry the casket. It is considered a great honor to be a pallbearer. The Talmud illustrates the importance of the *mitzvah* when it says (Ketubbot 17a): "One must abandon the study of Torah to carry the dead [to their resting place]." The practice of family and friends carrying the deceased to the grave dates back to biblical times when Jacob's sons carried him into the land of Canaan and buried him there (Genesis 50:13). It is also quite common for the coffin to be placed on a special cemetery wagon and wheeled to the gravesite.

As an indication of our reluctance to take leave of our loved one forever, the procession pauses several times on the way to the gravesite. Seven stops are traditional, but this number may vary.

During the procession Psalm 91 is recited. This beautiful psalm, which is also known as the "Song of the Spirit," expresses confidence that God will watch over us.

Upon reaching the grave, a prayer called *Tzidduk Ha-Din* (Hebrew for "submission to Divine judgment") is often recited. *Tzidduk Ha-Din* acknowledges God's judgment and righteousness, it asks for God's mercy, and it accepts the inevitability of death as part of the Divine plan. *Tzidduk Ha-Din* is not recited when the somber theme of the prayer is incompatible with the spirit of certain holidays, such as Ḥannukah and Purim. Another prayer is then substituted.

The customs surrounding the interment vary within each branch of Judaism. The coffin is lowered into the grave by hand or by mechanical device. The earth is shoveled onto the coffin. It is considered both a duty and an honor to help in filling the grave. As this is done, the shovel is usually not passed directly from one person to the

Lowering the Coffin into the Grave.   *Prague, ca. 1780.*

next but is placed on the ground before being picked up each time. This gesture symbolizes the hope that the tragedy of death will not pass from one person to another. It also symbolizes the desire not to rush this final parting from the deceased.

Some families prefer not to be present for the lowering of the coffin. They may wish to place several handfuls of earth on the coffin, which is then lowered after the mourners leave.

There is some variation in the final prayers recited at graveside. Sometimes the *El Malei Raḥamim* is said, sometimes Psalm 49. A special burial *Kaddish* may replace the Mourner's *Kaddish*.

Upon leaving the cemetery, Jews traditionally form two lines and, as the bereaved pass between them, they recite the words: "May the Lord comfort you among the other mourners of Zion and Jerusalem" *("Ha-makom yenaḥem etkhem betokh she'ar avelei Tzion vi'Yerushalayim")*. This custom marks the family's transition into a state of formal mourning. The focus has changed from honoring the deceased to comforting the mourners.

Private rituals have developed over many years. For example, some Jews pull up a few blades of grass as they leave the cemetery. This was originally done as an expression of faith in resurrection. Just as the plucked grass would grow once more, so would we and our loved ones live again. Another explanation is that it is done to illustrate the transient nature of life.

Some wash their hands upon leaving the cemetery as a symbol of purification after being in contact with the dead. This washing may also be done upon entering the house of mourning.

Reciting Kaddish

The prayer we call *Kaddish* appears in every worship service. There are five variations of the basic *Kaddish*, one of them the Mourner's *Kaddish*. This prayer is one of the most beautiful in Judaism, and many find its words a comfort when they are sorrowful. The cadences are important for the bereaved even when the meaning of specific words may not be known.

"One generation goes, another comes,

but the world remains forever."

ECCLESIASTES 1:4

The *Kaddish* is an ancient prose-poem that developed over a period of centuries. Among its earlier purposes was to separate parts of the service. With the exception of the last verse, which is in Hebrew, the *Kaddish* is written in Aramaic, the language spoken by our people in the time of Ezra in the fifth century B.C.E. and for many centuries thereafter.

Kaddish is an Aramaic word meaning "sanctification." It is related to the Hebrew word *kadosh* ("holy"). Though most versions of the *Kaddish* contain no mention of death, the *Kaddish* came to be recited by mourners during the thirteenth century. It praises God, affirms God's holiness, and anticipates the establishment of peace on earth. At the very moment when our faith may be most tested, we praise God, our Creator, and we pray for the unification and completion of a world we feel is fragmented.

The words of the *Kaddish* create a fellowship with others who have suffered loss. It is said in the presence of a public quorum of ten adults (in Hebrew, *minyan*). When a parent dies, one recites *Kaddish* for eleven months. In theory, mourning for parents continues for twelve months, but traditional Jews consider a full year to be

the duration required for judgment of the wicked. Since we do not view our parents as wicked, we demonstrate this fact by saying *Kaddish* for eleven months only. Many Jews say it for a full year, retaining the talmudic custom of mourning.

MOURNERS' KADDISH

Yitgadal v'yitkadash sh'mei raba	יִתְגַּדַּל וְיִתְקַדַּשׁ שְׁמֵהּ רַבָּא
b'alma di v'ra ckir'utei,	בְּעָלְמָא דִּי בְרָא כִרְעוּתֵהּ,
v'yamlikh malkhutei b'ḥayeikhon	וְיַמְלִיךְ מַלְכוּתֵהּ בְּחַיֵּיכוֹן
u-v'yomeikhon, u-v'ḥayei d'khol	וּבְיוֹמֵיכוֹן, וּבְחַיֵּי דְכָל
beit yisrael, ba-agala	בֵּית יִשְׂרָאֵל, בַּעֲגָלָא
u-vi-z'man kariv, v'imru amen.	וּבִזְמַן קָרִיב, וְאִמְרוּ אָמֵן.
Y'hei sh'mei raba m'varakh	יְהֵא שְׁמֵהּ רַבָּא מְבָרַךְ
l'alam u-l'almei almaya.	לְעָלַם וּלְעָלְמֵי עָלְמַיָּא.
Yitbarakh v'yishtabaḥ v'yitpa'ar	יִתְבָּרַךְ וְיִשְׁתַּבַּח, וְיִתְפָּאַר
v'yitromam, v'yitnasei, v'yit-hadar,	וְיִתְרוֹמַם, וְיִתְנַשֵּׂא וְיִתְהַדָּר,
v'yit'aleh v'yit'halal sh'mei	וְיִתְעַלֶּה וְיִתְהַלָּל שְׁמֵהּ
d'kudsha, b'rikh hu,	דְּקֻדְשָׁא, בְּרִיךְ הוּא,
l'ela min kol birkhata	לְעֵלָּא מִן כָּל בִּרְכָתָא
v'shirata, tushb'vata v'neḥemata,	וְשִׁירָתָא, תֻּשְׁבְּחָתָא וְנֶחֱמָתָא,
da-amiran b'alma, v'imru amen.	דַּאֲמִירָן בְּעָלְמָא, וְאִמְרוּ אָמֵן.
Y'hei sh'lama raba min sh'maya,	יְהֵא שְׁלָמָא רַבָּא מִן שְׁמַיָּא,
v'ḥayim aleinu v'al	וְחַיִּים, עָלֵינוּ וְעַל
kol Yisrael, v'imru amen.	כָּל יִשְׂרָאֵל, וְאִמְרוּ אָמֵן.
Oseh shalom bi-m'romav,	עֹשֶׂה שָׁלוֹם בִּמְרוֹמָיו,
hu ya'aseh shalom aleinu	הוּא יַעֲשֶׂה שָׁלוֹם עָלֵינוּ
v'al kol Yisrael, v'imru amen.	וְעַל כָּל יִשְׂרָאֵל, וְאִמְרוּ אָמֵן.

Glorified and hallowed be the great name of God throughout the world which was created according to Divine will. May the rule of peace be established speedily in our time, unto us and unto the entire household of Israel. Amen.

May God's great name be praised throughout all eternity. Extolled and glorified, honored and adored, ever be the name of the Holy One. God is beyond the praises and hymns of glory which mortals offer throughout the world. Amen.

May there be a great heavenly peace and life unto us, unto all Israel. Amen.

May the One who ordains the harmony of the universe, bestow peace upon us and upon the whole house of Israel. Amen.

Kaddish is usually recited for a thirty-day period for other close relatives—son, daughter, brother, sister, and spouse—although sometimes individuals choose to extend the *Kaddish* period beyond thirty days. *Kaddish* is also said each year on the anniversary of the death of a loved one (*yahrzeit*) and at *Yizkor* services (memorial services held during certain holiday periods).

Typically, mourners say *Kaddish* toward the end of the service. In many congregations there is an additional *Kaddish* for mourners after the Morning Blessings.

Traditionally only the mourners stand during *Kaddish*. At the last verse, they take three steps back, symbolizing the end of their audience with God, then three steps forward to their original position. In many congregations *all* the worshippers rise as a sign of respect to the memory of the departed. The entire congregation shows its support and solidarity with the mourners and its remembrance of the victims of the Holocaust who left no one behind to say *Kaddish* for them.

Reciting the *Kaddish* in memory of our beloved dead brings us all closer as our voices rhythmically echo all those who have mourned before us. In that moment we form a community which transcends death.

A Period of Mourning

The First Week: Shiva

A period of mourning begins immediately after the burial. In Jewish law this mourning process is divided into stages designed to ease the mourner back into the mainstream of life.

Shiva is the initial phase of deepest mourning. It is usually observed for a seven-day period. This intense period of mourning provides an opportunity for the close relatives of the deceased—parent, spouse, child, or sibling—to begin the process of recovery by concentrating on their grief. They remain at home and receive visitors who come to express sympathy and love. The mourners are not left alone; they are surrounded by people who care and share their loss. The visitors also help form a *minyan* for prayer services in the house of mourning.

···

"There is a time to weep . . ."

···

ECCLESIASTES 3:4

The practice of *shiva* (Hebrew for "seven") probably dates back to biblical times. When the Patriarch Jacob died, his son Joseph "wailed with a very great and sore wailing, and he made a mourning for his father seven days" (Genesis 50:10). The Rabbis of the Talmud specified "three days for weeping and seven for lamenting" (Moed Katan 27b). From this we deduce that the first three days of *shiva* are the most intense. It is for this reason that some Jews observe *shiva* for three days only.

Jewish tradition considers a fraction of a day as a complete day. Therefore the day of burial is considered a full day of mourning, even if the interment takes place late in the afternoon. Similarly, the seventh day is regarded as a full day although mourning is observed for only a short time after sunrise. Shabbat is counted as one of the seven days, but there are no public signs of mourning on this day. On Shabbat, ribbons or torn garments are not worn, and mourners attend synagogue services. The bereaved return to their formal state of mourning at home on Saturday night after Shabbat has ended.

Usually the *shiva* period ends on the morning of the seventh day after burial, immediately following the morning prayer service *(Shabarit)*. At that time the mourners rise from their week of mourning.

"God heals the broken-hearted and

binds up their wounds."

PSALM 147:3

The timing and duration of mourning are affected by the holidays of Passover, Shavuot, Sukkot, Rosh Hashanah, and Yom Kippur. The general rule is that these Jewish holidays cancel the *shiva*. So, for example, if mourning begins on a Wednesday and a festival starts that night, the remainder of the *shiva* is nullified. Those few hours of *shiva* observance are regarded as the equivalent of seven full days. Another example: if someone dies on the first day of Shavuot, the burial takes place on the morning *after* Shavuot. Shiva begins then and lasts for seven days. If, however, the funeral takes place on an intermediate day of a festival *(Hol Ha-Moed)*, the period of *shiva* does not begin until after the festival ends. The procedure for holidays that fall during the *shiva* period can be complicated. It is best to consult your rabbi if this situation occurs.

How Shiva Is Observed

Shiva is observed in the home of the deceased or at a close relative's house.

When the mourners return from the cemetery, a special candle is lit, which burns for the entire *shiva* period. This *shiva* candle is commonly provided by the funeral director. In Proverbs 20:27 we read: "The human soul is the light of God." The candlelight symbolizes the soul of the deceased as well as the presence of God. It is a sign of respect to the memory of the deceased.

The mourners eat a meal of condolence (in Hebrew, *seudat havra'ah*) when they return from the cemetery. It often includes hard-boiled eggs, the symbol of fertility and life, and bread, the staff of life in Judaism. The meal is usually provided by friends and neighbors. Jewish tradition considers the bringing of food to mourning friends and relatives a *mitzvah* and an expression of consolation. Throughout the

Group Portrait of Members of the Burial Society. *Prague, ca. 1780.*

shiva period it is likely that friends will bring or send platters of food, thus helping to free the mourners from some everyday concerns. While it is acceptable to drink wine or liquor at the house of mourning, it should not be for the purpose of merriment or the avoidance of reality.

It is traditional for mirrors to be covered in the house where *shiva* is observed. This practice symbolizes withdrawal from worldly concerns and from the importance of personal appearance. Many Jews, however, do not cover the mirrors in the house of mourning.

Traditionally, mourners do not sit on chairs of normal height. Instead they sit close to the ground on low stools or benches. This practice may account for the expression "sitting *shiva*." It is probably based on the biblical reference to Job, whose three friends came to comfort him and "for seven days and seven nights they sat beside him on the ground" (Job 2:13). The chair need not necessarily be uncomfortable, as long as it is lower than normal. Mourners need not *sit* all the time during *shiva*. They may stand, walk, or lie down to rest. When sitting, the mourner does not rise from his or her chair to greet any visitor, no matter how important that person may be.

An integral part of *shiva* is the condolence call. It is a *mitzvah* to visit a house of mourning during that time. In Hebrew this act is called *niḥum avelim* or "comforting mourners." The Talmud teaches that consoling mourners is an act of God (Sotah 14a). One of the first examples of an actual condolence call is when Job's friends "sat with him and none spoke to him for they saw that his suffering was very great" (Job 2:13).

The purpose of the condolence call is to offer companionship to the mourners— to offer support and a sympathetic ear. Small talk and socializing are discouraged; rather, visitors should speak about the deceased and encourage the mourners to express their feelings. It is likely that the mourners will experience mood swings; laughter over funny or dear memories may alternate with tears and anger.

Visitors usually do not bring flowers or gifts other than food. Instead they often make donations to charity in the name of the deceased.

During the *shiva* period the mourner does not leave the house and does not work, except if severe financial loss will result. Some Jews do not wear leather shoes during *shiva*; these are replaced by canvas or other soft shoes. This is done in a spirit of self-denial and humility, since leather is viewed as a luxury.

Daily prayer services are held in the home of the deceased. These services take place in the presence of a *minyan* so that the mourner may recite *Kaddish*. The services may be held in the morning and/or evening, traditionally for the week of *shiva*, but sometimes for one or three days. Various changes may be made in the regular prayer service when it is held in a house of mourning. Prayer booklets for this purpose are usually available at the funeral home or from the synagogue. The pattern of services in the home may depend on family tradition or the customs of your synagogue.

When mourners go to the synagogue on the first Shabbat following a loved one's death, they are usually greeted with the words, "May God comfort you along with all the mourners of Zion and Jerusalem."

It is traditional for mourners to end the *shiva* period by taking a walk around the block to symbolize their return to a more normal life. Some of the prayer booklets include prayers and directions for this brief ritual.

The First Month: Sheloshim

Sheloshim (Hebrew for "thirty") is a thirty-day period of mourning that begins immediately after the burial. When Moses died, the Children of Israel mourned him for thirty days (Deuteronomy 34:8). *Sheloshim* includes the *shiva* period and constitutes the full period of mourning for all relatives except parents, who are mourned for eleven or twelve months. However, some do mourn longer than thirty days for relatives other than parents.

The last twenty-three days of *sheloshim* are less restrictive than the seven days of *shiva*. Mourners may return to work but generally do not attend social gatherings or participate in festive events. *Kaddish* is recited daily at the synagogue. Many Jews do not have haircuts or shave during this period.

Just as in *shiva*, the observance of *sheloshim* is affected by the Jewish holidays. It is best to consult your rabbi if a festival falls during these thirty days.

Those who sat *shiva* in a community other than their own (for example, where their parent lived) or whose *shiva* was very brief because of a festival may want to hold a *minyan* at their home to mark the end of *sheloshim* in order to receive the comfort of their community.

Unveiling the Gravestone

The gravestone, or monument, may be erected at the end of *shiva* or up to twelve months after death. The purpose of the tombstone is to mark the gravesite clearly and permanently.

The monument (in Hebrew, *matzevah*) is usually selected soon after the funeral. The tombstone is simple and can be made of stone or metal. It may lie horizontally or be erected vertically. The inscription on the stone usually contains a short

Hebrew phrase or a Jewish symbol, the Hebrew and English name of the deceased, and the Jewish and secular dates of birth and death.

"God has given,

and God has taken away;

Blessed be the name of God."

JOB 1:21

While in many parts of the world there is no formal ceremony of dedication, it is customary in the United States to dedicate the tombstone in a graveside ceremony called an unveiling. The unveiling, which is the formal removal of a veil or other covering over the tombstone, symbolizes the official erection of the monument. Immediate family and close friends usually attend the dedication ceremony, which is accompanied by a brief service in memory of the person who has died. A rabbi usually officiates at this ceremony, although a rabbi's presence is not required in Jewish tradition. Several psalms are recited and a few words are spoken about the deceased. The cloth is removed, the *El Malei Raḥamim* is chanted, and the *Kaddish* is recited.

The unveiling ceremony is often used to mark the end of the mourning period. In any event the occasion should be simple and include only the closest family and friends.

Remembrance

An Annual Memorial

Yahrzeit marks the anniversary of a death. The word is derived from Yiddish and means "year's time." It is traditionally observed according to the Hebrew date of death. If a parent dies on the tenth day of Kislev, 5752, *yahrzeit* is observed on the tenth day of Kislev, 5753, and on that Hebrew date every year. However, some Jews follow the secular calendar.

Most Jews light a *yahrzeit* candle to commemorate the day. The candle is lit at sunset on the evening before the anniversary and is allowed to burn itself out. These commemorative candles are available in synagogue gift shops, Judaica stores, supermarkets, and grocery stores specializing in kosher foods. There are no standard prayers or prescribed blessings to accompany the lighting of the candle. One may recite any of the Psalms related to the funeral service (Psalms 15, 16, 23, 42,

49, 90, 91, 144) or one's own prayers, readings, and reflections. This can be an opportunity to read the Psalms carefully and choose one or more that are particularly appropriate to your emotions at the time. Special prayers and meditations on lighting a *yahrzeit* candle are found in many prayer books.

On the Shabbat before *yahrzeit* (or on other days when the Torah is read) the mourner may be called up to the Torah for an *aliyah*. The *aliyah* is considered a special honor. *Kaddish* is recited on the day of *yahrzeit* or on the preceding Shabbat. Before *Kaddish*, the rabbi may read the names of the deceased whose *yahrzeit* is observed during that week. If the deceased's name is on the synagogue's memorial plaque, a bulb will often be lit next to it.

It is customary to visit the cemetery on or close to this anniversary. Many people perform the *mitzvah* of giving *tzedakah* to commemorate the *yahrzeit*. They may also engage in other acts of special kindness at this time.

Yizkor: *May God Remember*

A memorial service called *Yizkor* (Hebrew for "may God remember") is held in the synagogue on major Jewish holidays: Yom Kippur, Shemini Atzeret, and the last days of Passover and Shavuot. *Yizkor* usually takes place in the morning after the Torah service. Many Jews light a memorial candle on the eve before *Yizkor* is said.

It is believed that *Yizkor* was introduced into the worship services during the massacres of the Christian Crusades and medieval pogroms (twelfth century). A memorial service would be held on Yom Kippur to honor those Jews who were killed. Subsequently *Yizkor* became a service to remember Jewish martyrs and our own deceased loved ones as well. During the eighteenth century *Yizkor* came to be recited four times a year rather than once on Yom Kippur.

Yizkor is recited beginning on the first holiday after the death. Some congregants leave the synagogue during *Yizkor* if their parents are living, but doing so is *not* required in Jewish practice. In synagogues where all congregants remain throughout this service, *Kaddish* may be recited for friends or relatives who have died, or in memory of Jewish martyrs.

Yizkor is the first word of the Memorial Prayer (*Hazkarat Neshamot*). One prayer may be said for all one's deceased, naming each person in the blank spaces indicated, or an individual prayer may be recited for each one. *El Malei Raḥamim*, *Kaddish*, and other prayers may also be recited.

Yizkor is an opportunity for making contributions in the name of the deceased to perpetuate their memories and to promote the values they held.

Visiting the Grave

Judaism discourages frequent grave visitation, for it may hinder the mourner's return to normal life. However, there are days when it is traditional to visit the cemetery. These include the days before the High Holy Days and special personal days such as birthdays and anniversaries.

Several blessings and psalms may be recited at the graveside, including the memorial prayer *El Malei Rahamim*.

Visitors to the grave often leave a small stone on the tombstone as a symbol of the enduring bond between the visitor and the deceased. It is an act of love, a gesture to show that you were there.

P • A • R • T

2

The Rhythm of Our Year:
A Guide to the Jewish Holidays

THE FALL HOLIDAYS

THE SPRING HOLIDAYS

SHABBAT

The Fall Holidays

"Wholeness and holiness we seek

as we enter a new year"

———

RABBINICAL ASSEMBLY
MAHZOR

Days of Awe

For centuries the High Holy Days have captivated the Jewish people with a mysterious and inescapable bond. The call of the shofar on Rosh Hashanah rouses us from summer drowsiness, giving us a fresh supply of spiritual energy at a time when we seem to need it most. For the next ten days we feel ourselves drawing closer to God, until we reach the spiritual heights of Yom Kippur. It is a time of reflection: a time to reflect on the past, to marvel at the wonders of God's world, and to think about what we want ourselves and our children to become.

A thorough housecleaning is traditional and, because we want to be seen in our best light during this "time of judgment," new clothes help set these days apart as a special time.

In the weeks before Rosh Hashanah many people visit the graves of loved ones. This custom helps us consider our past as we prepare for a new year.

A medieval poet wrote, "On Rosh Hashanah it is written, and on Yom Kippur it is sealed." These words, which we recite during the Rosh Hashanah morning service, tie the two holidays together with a powerful image. Tradition says that on Rosh Hashanah God writes judgments in the Book of Life, but the book remains open until Yom Kippur. During these ten days of repentance, we have the opportunity through prayer, the performance of *mitzvot* (righteous acts), and the resolve to become better people, to influence God's judgment—that is, to be "Sealed in the Book of Life." We can then let go of the old year and the mistakes we made. Taking our children by the hand, we step together into the New Year.

Rosh Hashanah

The Hebrew words *Rosh Hashanah* mean "head of the year," and this day, the first of the Hebrew month Tishre, marks the beginning of the Jewish year. It also celebrates the creation of the world, for Jewish tradition tells us that God completed the seven days of Creation on Rosh Hashanah. Rosh Hashanah has several other names and meanings as well. From the Torah, it is *Yom Teruah*, the Day of Sounding the Shofar, a reminder of the covenant between God and the Jewish people. It is *Yom Ha-Zikaron*, a "Day of Remembering," a time to review the past year, considering both the good we have done and the times when we did not measure up. It is also *Yom Ha-Din*, the "Day of Judgment." The Jewish tradition holds that we are evenly balanced: part good, part sinful. Thus one righteous act, one *mitzvah*, can tip the scales in our favor, and we can be inscribed in the Book of Life.

At Home

Rosh Hashanah, like all Jewish holidays, begins in the evening. The Book of Nehemiah tells us how to celebrate the first night: "Eat rich food and drink sweet wine, and share with those who have none" 8:10. Before the meal, the home festival service includes reciting the blessing over the candles, the *Sheheḥeyanu* (a blessing for special occasions), the festival *Kiddush* over wine, and the blessing over bread, *Ha-Motzi* (see pages 142, 143).

Customs and Traditions

Rather than the traditional oval braided bread, the ḥallah for Rosh Hashanah is round, representing our cyclical sense of time. As one year ends and another begins, we come full circle like a wheel. Some sources liken the round *ḥallah* to a majestic crown, a symbol of God's sovereignty. We eat the *ḥallah* with apple slices dipped in honey to express our hope for a sweet year.

Generations of Jews have greeted each other with the traditional Rosh Hashanah refrain: "May you be inscribed for a good year!" In the last century, as families spread out over larger distances, people began sending these greetings through the mail on Rosh Hashanah cards. "*Shanah Tovah*—A Good Year!"

In the Synagogue

The focus of Rosh Hashanah is the synagogue rather than the home. This time of remembrance and judgment affects us not as individuals, but as a community.

The themes of creation, remembrance, and redemption are echoed throughout the Rosh Hashanah liturgy. In our prayers we acknowledge God's sovereignty and we recognize our human failings.

"And in that day a great shofar will sound."

ISAIAH 27:13

The most striking aspect of the Rosh Hashanah services is the sounding of the shofar. This is the biblical injunction for the celebration of Rosh Hashanah: *In the seventh month, on the first day of the month, you shall observe a sacred occasion. You shall not work at your occupations. You shall observe it as a day when the shofar is sounded.* (Numbers 29:1)

The shofar has inspired many interpretations. The Rabbis of talmudic times heard the shofar as a sign of God's mercy. Maimonides, the great Jewish philosopher, heard it as a call to repentance.

The Bible cites the shofar in a variety of contexts. It was blown to announce the New Moon and to sound an alarm in times of crisis. For the prophet Isaiah it hailed the coming of the messianic age.

It is a thrilling fanfare, calling to mind ancient times and reminding us of our covenant with God at Sinai.

The sounding of the shofar follows a specific pattern that incorporates four distinct sounds. In Hebrew, these are:

> *tekiah*, one long blast
> *teruah*, nine staccato blasts
> *shevarim*, three short blasts
> *tekiah gedolah*, one very long blast

Tashlikh

In the afternoon after Rosh Hashanah services, many people go to a nearby river or other body of flowing water and throw crumbs into the waters, symbolic of ridding themselves of their sins. "You will cast your sins into the depths of the sea" (Micah 7:19). The *Tashlikh* ceremony, a refreshing outdoor contrast to the morning hours spent in the synagogue, helps us make a fresh start for the New Year.

··

"Renew us for a year that is

good and sweet."

··

ROSH HASHANNAH LITURGY

Rosh Hashanah for Children

Although young children are not able to sit through long services, there are many ways to share the message of the holiday with children of all ages. Most synagogues now incorporate children's services into their Rosh Hashanah schedule. Of course, all children can participate in home activities. Making New Year's cards to send to friends and relatives is a particularly nice family project, and those with a flair for kitchen activities can try baking honey cake or making *taiglach*, a traditional honey candy (see recipe page 157).

Yom Kippur

More than anything else, Yom Kippur is about forgiveness. On Rosh Hashanah we began to review our shortcomings and successes of the past year. The days that follow provide the opportunity to apologize for our errors and seek forgiveness from those we may have wronged. This is *teshuvah*, or repentance. It is only after we have worked out our grievances among ourselves, forgiving and being forgiven by our families and friends, that we can then ask God's forgiveness. Yom Kippur is about our repentance and about God's mercy.

At Home

Yom Kippur is a solemn day, a day for thought and for prayer. Our focus is on the spiritual rather than the temporal, and to emphasize this, we fast from sundown to sundown. Fasting teaches us compassion. In our temporary deprivation, we remember that there are still people for whom hunger is present far more often than once a year. Fasting also points up our own human frailty and dependence upon God. A simple fact, but how easily we forget it: without food, we cannot live. Tradition requires adults to fast, but not young children, the elderly, or the sick.

The eve of Yom Kippur is ushered in with a hearty meal. After the table is cleared, and we set off for evening services, we light a *yahrzeit* candle in remembrance of family members who are no longer alive. This memorial candle burns throughout Yom Kippur. Yom Kippur candles also are lit and the blessing is recited (see page 142). Some families spread a clean tablecloth and set out books in place of plates, to show that Yom Kippur is a day for study and contemplation rather than feasting and festivities. Finally, it is customary for parents to bless their children (see page 126).

In the Synagogue

The evening service takes its name from the famous prayer *Kol Nidre*, noted for its sad yet beautiful melody. Written in Aramaic, it is traditionally sung by the cantor. In *Kol Nidre* we ask for God's understanding and forgiveness for the vows we made to God that we are unable to keep. A vow is a holy promise and we need forgiveness if we break it.

"Forgive and pardon our sins

on this Day of Atonement."

YOM KIPPUR CONFESSIONAL

On the following day the service is very long. In the *Al Ḥet* prayer we confess our sins as a congregation, accepting responsibility not only for our own misdeeds, but for those of our family and community as well. Also included a number of times during Yom Kippur services is the *Avinu Malkenu* ("Our Parent, our Ruler"), a prayer asking God to forgive us despite our failings.

Yom Kippur services include *Yizkor*, the memorial service for the dead, and two Torah readings. During the afternoon service we read the Book of Jonah, with its story of the people of an evil city who repent their ways and are forgiven by God.

The concluding service of Yom Kippur is *Ne'ilah*, from *Ne'ilat Ha-Sh'arim* or the closing of the gates. Some rabbis thought this referred to the closing of the Temple gates; others have said it refers to the gates of heaven, closing as the Book of Life is sealed. *Ne'ilah* ends with one last blast of the shofar and the cry, "Next year in Jerusalem!"

Jonah and the Whale.

From an Arabic manuscript, 1306

At the close of the *Ne'ilah* service, some synagogues invite their congregants to break the fast together with a light snack. Later, at home, we enjoy a special meal shared with family and friends, perhaps inviting people who would otherwise be alone. It is a joyful evening after a long and solemn day. We feel reinvigorated for the year that lies ahead.

Tzedakah

The message of Yom Kippur goes beyond repentance and forgiveness. As we look back on the mistakes of the past year, we think about how to improve ourselves. But as Jews, we also ask ourselves how we can improve the world. This is the spirit of *tzedakah*, the way we help others. In the synagogue it may mean special fund-raising drives to support the United Jewish Appeal or other charitable organizations. At home it can mean any special effort or project to aid people less fortunate than ourselves.

Yom Kippur for Children

Even young children can be guided to an understanding of the message of repentance, forgiveness, and change for the better, which are the hallmarks of Yom Kippur. Many synagogues offer special children's or family services. Obviously, fasting is not appropriate for young children, but they might want to make a partial attempt, skipping a meal or not eating candy or snacks.

Consider a family *tzedakah* project. Your children can save money to give to the poor. Together, you can visit someone who is ill, or volunteer in a soup kitchen. Activities like these help to teach children that when we become better people, we can help to make the world a better place.

Sukkot

The Bible calls Sukkot *"The Festival."* Already ancient by the time of King Solomon, it was one of the most important holidays of the year. In the fall, with the harvest safely stored, the Israelites commenced a week-long celebration of thanksgiving. Many went on pilgrimage to Jerusalem. There they stayed in makeshift little huts which eventually lent their name, *sukkot*, to the festival itself.

Later generations saw a symbolic connection between those huts and the tents of the Israelites in the Sinai wilderness. For them the holiday became a reminder of our ultimate dependence on God. Today we build big sturdy houses and buy our food in supermarkets, but once a year we sit in a fragile little *sukkah*, open to wind and sky, and remember our own limitations.

Many commentators linked the *sukkot* to the huts built by our ancestors at harvest time. These farmers had to work continuously lest the produce rot in the fields, so they built little huts close to their fields and worked from first light to darkness.

Today we sit in the *sukkah* at our leisure. In the pleasant evening air, we sing and eat in the *sukkah*, lingering as long as the weather permits. Some people even sleep overnight in their *sukkah*.

At Home

The Rabbis gave detailed instructions to *sukkah* builders. A *sukkah* must have at least three walls. These can be made of the flimsiest of materials, even cloth, as long as it does not tear in strong wind. The roof is covered with leaves or branches, thick enough to give shade but sparse enough to let you see the stars at night. The structure is decorated with fruits, vegetables, artwork, or anything festive and special. The construction is done before the holidays; some families begin to build a *sukkah* right after breaking the fast on Yom Kippur.

"In order that future generations may know

that I made the Israelites live in sukkot

when I brought them out of Egypt."

LEVITICUS 23:42, 43

A mystical tradition holds that certain of our ancestors come to sit with us in the *sukkah*. They are called *ushpizin*—"holy guests." When we enter the *sukkah*, we stand in the doorway and greet them with an ancient welcome: "I invite to my meal, honored spiritual guests Abraham, Isaac, Jacob, Joseph, Moses, Aaron, and

The *sukkah* is a perfect instrument for delighting and instructing children. Those who bemoan the absence of a Christmas tree in Jewish tradition have probably never given the *sukkah* a thought.

David." In recent times some have expanded the list of *ushpizin* to include important women of the Bible: Sarah, Rachel, Rebecca, Leah, Miriam, Abigail, and Esther.

The *Zohar*, a collection of mystical lore, warns that the *ushpizin* will not join our celebration unless we also invite the poor. This teaching reminds us of the Jewish tradition of hospitality. Honor the *ushpizin* by inviting family, friends, and neighbors to your *sukkah*.

The holiday opens in the *sukkah* with the candle blessing, *Kiddush*, and *Ha-Motzi* (see pages 142, 143). The *Sheheheanu* blessing is added on the first night of the festival. Then comes a special blessing for Sukkot (see page 144) followed by a festival meal. Interestingly, there are no particular foods associated directly with *Sukkot*, but a dessert of apple strudel is a delicious excuse for sitting a little longer in the *sukkah*, enjoying the fruits of the fall (see page 158).

In the Synagogue

On Sukkot, the priests of the Second Temple performed an elaborately choreographed ritual. Our own festival observance preserves some of those ancient ceremonies.

For example, many Jews come to Sukkot morning services carrying a *lulav* and *etrog*, known collectively as the "four species." The *etrog* is a lemon-like fruit or citron. The *lulav* bundle contains three different types of tree twigs: palm, myrtle, and willow. Their use as ceremonial objects goes back to biblical times: "On the

In the synagogue on SImhat Torah every Torah is taken from the Ark and carried in a series of processions called *hakkafot*.

first day, you shall take the fruit of a goodly tree *(etrog)*, palm branches, thick boughs of trees (myrtle), and willows and rejoice before God" (Leviticus 23:40).

Some rabbis have likened each of the four species to different types of Jews; while held together they symbolize the unity of the Jewish people.

During the synagogue service the *lulav* is shaken in every direction—to the front, to the right, to the back, to the left, up, and down—demonstrating our recognition that God is everywhere.

The Eighth Day of Sukkot

Sukkot closes with the holiday of Shemini Atzeret, an "Assembly of the Eighth Day." Originally Shemini Atzeret was a day of meditation and rest. Like other holidays, Shemini Atzeret took on a second day in the Diaspora. By the eleventh century that second day had become a separate holiday—the irrepressible Simḥat Torah. In Liberal congregations Shemini Atzeret and Simḥat Torah are celebrated on the same day.

Sukkot for Children

The *sukkah* is a perfect instrument for delighting and instructing children. Building and decorating a *sukkah* can be a family project in which children of all ages can participate. Paper chains, drawings, paintings, and photographs, in addition to fruits and flowers, make colorful, lively additions to the *sukkah*. Some families save their Rosh Hashanah cards to hang in the *sukkah* as well. The length of the holiday also provides many opportunities for children to invite their own guests to join family meals in the *sukkah*.

Simḥat Torah

Simḥat Torah, translated as "rejoicing in the Torah," celebrates the annual cycle of Torah reading. On Simḥat Torah we finish the last portion of Deuteronomy and begin again with the first chapter of Genesis. The holiday could have evolved into a dry salute to scholarship, but it is instead a dancing and singing holiday, one that has been compared to a joyous wedding. It brings the Torah closer to all of us, scholar and nonscholar, adult and child.

In the Synagogue

Adults are called up to the Torah to chant the blessings, an *aliyah*. In some synagogues the last *aliyah* is given to all the children. A large *tallit*, prayer shawl, is held over their heads and everyone in the congregation chants the Torah blessings with them.

During the service, every Torah scroll is taken out of the Ark, or *Aron Ha-Kodesh*. Singing songs, everyone parades around the synagogue in a series of seven processions called *hakkafot*—"circlings." By the end of the last *hakkafah*, everyone who wants to has carried the Torah. Children wave flags and march along too. Some scholars have likened these flags to the twelve tribal banners of ancient Israel.

Simḥat Torah for Children

With its dancing, flag waving, and wonderful sense of abandon, Simḥat Torah is a holiday with particular appeal for children. They can make their own flags to wave, and the celebration is capped with jelly apples and other sweets.

Ḥanukkah

During the darkest season of the year, Ḥanukkah comes into our lives with a cheerful combination of games and gifts, songs and stories, light and laughter. It occurs near the winter solstice, when days are short but promise to lengthen once again. A hint of that promise comes from the Ḥanukkah candles, glowing warmly against the bleak background of deep winter.

Although Ḥannukah is the only major holiday that has no basis in the Bible, it is the best documented of all the Jewish holidays. Its story is so simple yet so powerful that it cannot fail to captivate even a young child. In 168 B.C.E. a small group of Jews, led by Judah "The Maccabee," rebelled against the Greek culture forced on them by the Syrian rulers. They refused to submit to the new order of Antiochus IV, King of Syria, who had outlawed many Jewish practices and placed idols in the Temple of Jerusalem. The Maccabees fought a bold campaign of guerrilla warfare, attacking and retreating to camps hidden in the Judean hills. Despite tremendous odds, they drove the Syrian-Greeks out of the land.

In the month of Kislev in the year 165 B.C.E. the Maccabees rededicated the Temple to Jewish worship. They then celebrated with an eight-day festival. The holiday's name, Ḥanukkah, comes from the Hebrew word for "dedication."

Five hundred years later the Rabbis of the Talmud reexamined the message of Ḥanukkah. Instead of emphasizing a military battle to keep Judaism alive, they spoke of God's miraculous way. When the Maccabees purified the Temple, the Talmud tells us, they found a small vial of oil for the Temple lamp, containing

Silver Ḥanukkah lamp.
Germany, 1824

enough to last only one day. Eight days later the menorah still burned! In recounting this miracle, the Rabbis lifted Ḥanukkah from its historical context. More than a commemoration of victory in war, Ḥanukkah now celebrated faith in God.

At Home

The menorah stands as the most compelling symbol of Ḥanukkah. In ancient times it stood in the Temple in Jerusalem, a symbol of Jewish peoplehood long before the Maccabees' revolt. The original seven-branched menorah is first mentioned in the Bible, but on Ḥanukkah we use one with nine branches, called a *ḥanukkiah*. Eight lights represent the eight days of the holiday, and the ninth, called the *shamash*, is used to light the others (see page 146).

A special song for Ḥanukkah is *Maoz Tzur* ("Rock of Ages"). For twenty-five generations or more, Jews have sung these words at Ḥanukkah after the lighting of the candles. When you sing *Maoz Tzur*, your voices join with theirs (see page 147).

Celebrating the miracle of the oil extends to food as well. Few of us can resist the delicious aroma and hearty flavor of latkes, the potato pancakes that are the holiday's enduring dish. It is also traditional during these festival days to indulge in doughnuts and other fried foods. A recipe for latkes begins on page 159.

Ḥanukkah for Children

After the candles are lit and the latkes are served, it's time for the special Ḥanukkah game, the dreidel game. Candy, nuts, raisins, or Ḥanukkah *gelt* (money) supply the "pot" in this traditional game from Eastern Europe.

To play, everyone puts some of their *gelt* into the pot. Each player spins the dreidel in turn. The four letters on the dreidel represent four different instructions in Yiddish:

נ , nun, for *nisht* (nothing). Player receives nothing.

ג , gimmel, for *ganz* (all). Player gets the whole pot.

ה , hay, for *halb* (half). Player gets half.

שׁ , shin, for *shtell* (put). Player contributes *gelt* to the pot.

There is also a Hebrew saying associated with the four letters. They stand for:

Nes Gadol Hayah Sham.

"A Great Miracle Happened There."

The practice of giving children small amounts of money, or *gelt*, for Ḥanukkah is an old Eastern European custom. It probably had its origins in the *tzedakah*, or charity, given to needy students at Ḥanukkah time so they could finish their Torah studies. In the United States Jews have expanded the custom of *gelt*-giving to a more elaborate exchange of gifts, adding a new layer of joy to an already happy holiday. Children might also choose a toy to donate to charity, thus emphasizing the special tradition of *tzedakah* in Judaism.

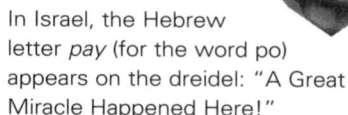

In Israel, the Hebrew letter *pay* (for the word po) appears on the dreidel: "A Great Miracle Happened Here!"

The Spring Holidays

"Blessed are You, Adonai our God,

Ruler of the world,

who has given us life, sustained us,

and brought us to this season."

———

SHEHEHEYANU

Tu B'Shevat

Winter is almost over and we eagerly await the first signs of spring. Daylight hours begin to lengthen, and before long the stark gray of the tree branches will be softened with misty green as new buds swell and new shoots seek out the warmth of the sun. It is time to celebrate Tu B'Shevat—the new year for trees.

The practical need for a "birthday" for trees arises from a Torah commandment: *"And when you come to the land and have planted all manner of trees for food, the fruit thereof shall be forbidden for three years; you shall not eat it. In the fourth year all the fruit thereof shall be holy and must be given to God. But in the fifth year you may eat the fruit, that it may yield unto you more richly the increase thereof."* (Leviticus 19:23-25)

In talmudic times the Rabbis chose the fifteenth day of the month of Shevat to mark the yearly aging of all trees. After the destruction of the Second Temple and the exile of Jews from their land, Tu B'Shevat also became a special link to Israel—a day to eat fruits associated with Eretz Yisrael. Later, as Jews began to return to settle in Israel during the late 1800s, they planted trees in order to revive the barren land, and Tu B'Shevat became a holiday for Jews all over the world to contribute to the greening of Israel.

············· ▬▬▬ ·············

"As the days of a tree, so shall be the

days of My People."

·········· ▬▬ ··········

Isaiah 65:22

At Home

Many Jews celebrate Tu B'Shevat with a special *seder* that features many Israeli fruits and four different kinds of wine.

The fruits fall into three groups: those without pits, shells, or inedible peel, such as figs, raisins, grapes, and berries; those with pits but no shells or peel, such as olives, plums, and dates; and those with outer layers that must be removed, such as oranges, grapefruits, almonds, and pomegranates.

Although the order of the ritual often varies, the seder itself consists of "courses" of each type of fruit, each course followed by a cup of wine. The first cup of wine is red, the second is red with a few drops of white, the third is white with a little red, and the fourth cup is white wine. A blessing for the Tu B'Shevat *seder* is on page 145. A recipe for schnecken, little fruit and nut morsels, is on page 160.

Tree Planting

In Israel Tu B'Shevat is a national holiday celebrated with tree-planting ceremonies. For over ninety years the Jewish National Fund has planted trees in Israel

The Jewish National Fund has planted over 200 million trees in Israel.

with contributions from Jews around the world. Through the J.N.F. we can plant trees to commemorate special events or special people. A tradition has developed to plant trees in honor of a new baby, in honor of a relative or friend who becomes Bar or Bat Mitzvah, or in memory of someone who dies.

Tu B'Shevat for Children

Making a family contribution to the Jewish National Fund or planting a tree in one's own yard are special and natural ways to celebrate Tu B'Shevat. Young children, however, may also enjoy a project with more immediacy. Simple indoor gardens can capture their imagination as they watch green shoots breaking through the black earth. Bean sprouts or alfalfa are good choices because they sprout quickly. Or you may wish to grow your own parsley to use for the coming Passover *seder*. Some synagogues have a formal tree planting on their grounds as part of the festivities of the holiday.

Tu B'Shevat is also a time to consider our more general connection to the earth and our obligation to take care of it. The Jewish tradition of *tikkun olam*—repairing the world—can be taken in an ecological as well as a spiritual sense. On this day, then, we can renew our commitment to this philosophy by planning a family recycling project.

Purim

We make noise in the synagogue, we parade in costumes, and we let the children stay up late. It's Purim and it's time to bend the rules.

The Purim story, though full of melodrama, plot twists, and palace intrigue, stresses themes of Jewish unity and courage in the face of anti-Semitism. Esther, the young Jewish queen of Persian King Ahasuerus, risked her life to convince the monarch not to allow his evil advisor Haman to kill the Jews.

An ambitious man, Haman tried to play upon fear of the Jews to consolidate his own power. He cited the classic argument of anti-Semites: "They follow different laws and customs from everyone else." He appealed to human greed, urging Persians to kill the Jews and take their possessions.

The Purim story also demonstrates the importance of courage. King Ahasuerus did not hate the Jews, nor did most of his subjects. But neither did they care enough to save them. When Haman presented his terrible plan to kill the Jews, King Ahasuerus unthinkingly agreed. Haman, by a throw of the dice called "lots" (*purim*), chose the thirteenth of Adar as the day to eliminate the Jews. Only the efforts of Esther and her cousin Mordecai defeated Haman. Only the vigilance of these heroes thwarted the enemy and rescued the Jews of Persia. As a result, Haman was unable to murder the Jews and was himself hanged for his evil plot.

According to the Book of Esther, the Jews of Persia took up arms against their enemies. But today we celebrate Purim with humor, a most nonviolent weapon. We defeat our enemy Haman by laughing at him, drowning out his name in a sea of noise.

········•────•········

Make them days of feasting and

gladness, and of sending portions

one to another and gifts.

·······•───•·······

MEGILLAH ESTHER

At Home

The fanciful celebrations of Purim call for costumes and masks, Purim gifts and hamantashen.

The practice of dressing in costume on Purim began in Italy during the fifteenth century. Italian Jews were probably imitating the Mardi Gras Carnival, which occurs around the same time of year as Purim. In borrowing from another culture, Italian Jews were actually reclaiming an ancient tradition. Carnival and Purim may share the same ancestor, a festival of early spring celebrated by Jews as well as other

peoples of the ancient Near East. Later the Book of Esther gave the festival its distinctly Jewish flavor and moral overtones.

Let your creativity flow when you design costumes. You can turn your children and yourselves into kings and queens, cowboys and clowns. A costume alters our identity, shielding us from the world and its restrictive demands. From behind a mask we play with reality, adopting and dropping roles as we please.

Purim's most recognizable and edible symbol is hamantashen, triangular cookies enclosing poppy seed or fruit filling. Their shape reminds us of Haman's three-cornered hat. In Israel the confection is called *oznai Haman*, "Haman's ears."

Acts of Tzedakah

The Book of Esther records a letter sent by Mordecai to Jews throughout the Persian Empire. He proclaimed the fourteenth and fifteenth days of the month of Adar to be "days of feasting and joy, days for sending presents to one another and gifts to the poor." Today on Purim, as on many other holidays, we undertake charitable acts of *tzedakah*.

Also on Purim we put together special baskets of fruit, cookies, or other food, called *mishloah manot*, and send or take them to friends and relatives. In this way we fulfill Mordecai's edict and rejoice in the happiness of the day. A recipe for hamantashen, fruit-filled cookies in the shape of Haman's triangular hat, is on page 161. Hamantashen make a welcome addition to *mishloah manot*.

In the Synagogue

The Hebrew word *megillah* means a handwritten scroll. It can refer to any of five different texts, but when we say *The* Megillah, we are talking about only one: the Book of Esther, our source for the events of the Purim story. It is read publicly in the synagogue during the Purim evening and morning services.

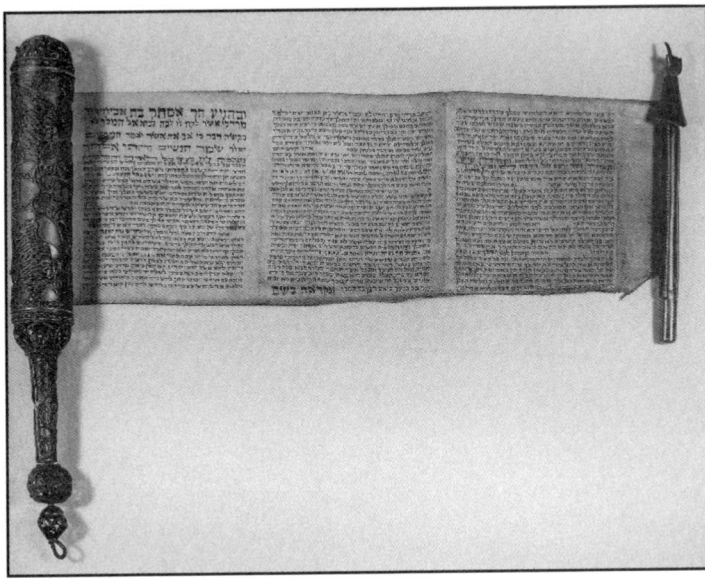

Scroll of Esther in ivory case. Nineteenth century.

We don't know if the events in the Book of Esther really happened. (In fact, unlike Ḥanukkah, there is no historical evidence in support of the Purim story, and some of its details conflict with historians' knowledge of Persia.) Nevertheless, we enjoy the Megillah simply for its exciting story. Thanks to a skillful anonymous writer, the book reads almost like a modern suspense novel.

Everyone participates in the Megillah reading. At every mention of Haman's name, we make as much noise as we can. We use *graggers* (the Yiddish name for noisemakers); we stamp our feet; we yell, hiss, and boo. We defeat Haman by laughing at him and drowning out the sound of his evil name.

Purim for Children

The silliness, the noisiness, the dressing up: Purim is a natural for children. Homemade *graggers* are a favorite Purim craft. Your children will certainly want to help plan their Purim costumes. Also they can create their own picture Megillah to take to synagogue.

Children are natural actors for your own *Purimshpiel* as well. *Shpiel* is the Yiddish word for "play." First introduced by German Jews in the late Middle Ages, a *Purimshpiel* retells the Purim story on stage. The actors often used humor to disguise sharp criticism of the community or government. You and your children can create your own *Purimshpiel*. You need not confine yourself to the story of Mordecai and Esther; touch on anything else you think funny or important. A successful *Purimshpiel* will entertain the whole family.

 # *P*assover

Children love to ask the question *why*. Our Rabbis knew that and built the observance of Passover, *Pesah*, around that very question. They also gave an answer, one that in two thousand years has not lost its power. When children ask the question, "How is this night different from all other nights?" they are answered with a retelling of the story of how we were freed from slavery in Egypt.

••••••••••••••◆◆◆•••••••••••••

"All people in every generation, must regard

themselves as having been

personally freed from Egypt"

•••••◆◆◆•••••

HAGGADAH

We retell the Passover story in the warm, inviting atmosphere of a family feast—the *seder*. The Rabbis designed the seder as a way of passing Jewish identity and awareness from parents to their children, from generation to generation. In fact, the

"Searching for Leaven," drawing by Bernard Picart. Holland, eighteenth century.

name of the book containing the *seder* service, Haggadah, means "telling." It comes from the biblical phrase, "And you shall tell your child."

Passover celebrates beginnings. We look out the window and see new green shoots budding on the trees, and we know that spring is here once again. The green vegetable or parsley on the *seder* plate symbolizes this seasonal rebirth.

Passover celebrates another beginning; our beginning as a free and independent people. The Book of Exodus captures those distant yet familiar events: The Book of Exodus captures those distant yet familiar events: Moses' confrontations with Pharaoh; the ten plagues; the hurried departure of the Hebrew slaves; the miraculous parting of the Sea of Reeds (the Red Sea). We are entranced by the drama and emotional content of the story, but we find it more difficult to understand that *we* were those Hebrews enslaved in Egypt. At the Passover *seder* we put ourselves inside that story by performing ritual acts—dipping greens in salt water or spilling drops of wine.

At Home

Early in the *seder* the Haggadah issues its famous invitation: "Let all who are hungry come and eat." Although we remember these words throughout the year, we heed them with special attention at Passover. Before the start of the holiday it is traditional to give *tzedakah*. This gift of charity is called *maot ḥittim*, "money for wheat," because it enables poor families to buy matzah and other foods for the holidays.

Generations of Jews have greeted Passover with strenuous housecleaning to remove all traces of *ḥametz* or leaven—the substance that makes dough rise. Jewish tradition provides the reason for this spring cleaning. When the Hebrew slaves heard that Pharaoh would permit them to leave Egypt, they packed hurriedly lest he change his mind. Carrying dough for bread on their backs, they let it bake in the desert sun. Later God commanded the people to remember their deliverance from Egypt each year by eating matzah and avoiding all *ḥametz*.

A tradition evolved that adds drama to the prohibition of *ḥametz*. On the night before the seder the family dims the lights and conducts a "search for leaven," *Bedikat Ḥametz*. Armed with a candle, a feather, a paper bag, and a wooden spoon, the family searches the house for those last remaining crumbs of bread. Because by this late hour most people have already finished their Passover cleaning, it became traditional to hide several pieces of *ḥametz* around the house prior to the search. If you do so, remember where you hide them, because you have to find every piece! In the morning, the *ḥametz* is burned outside the house. (For instructions, see page 151).

The Passover Seder

For centuries Jews commemorated the Exodus from Egypt with a pilgrimage to the Temple in Jerusalem. When the Temple was destroyed, our Rabbis developed new ways to keep the memory of the Exodus alive. One of these ways was the *seder*, a ritual meal modeled after the elaborate banquets of the Greeks. Later generations added other readings and songs and set the order down in a book called the Haggadah.

Complete instructions for making a *seder* can be found in the Haggadah; highlights are presented here to get you started.

The centerpiece of the *seder* table is the *seder* plate containing the five ritual foods of Passover:

Zeroah, the roasted lamb bone, reminds us of the Temple sacrifice.

Betzah, a roasted egg, is a symbol of the ancient festival offering as well as a reminder of spring and rebirth.

Maror, a bitter herb, traditionally horseradish, recalls the bitter taste of slavery.

Karpas, a green vegetable such as parsley, is another symbol of spring.

Ḥaroset reminds us of the brick mortar used by the Hebrew slaves. People of Eastern Europe make *ḥaroset* from apples, nuts, and wine. Sephardic Jews use other recipes containing dates, raisins, and figs, the fruits of Mediterranean lands.

A separate plate of matzah, three pieces covered with a cloth, sits nearby.

Every place setting at the *seder* table gets a wine glass, even the children's (though many people fill the children's glass with grape juice). During the *seder* we drink four cups of wine.

A pillow is placed on the *seder* leader's chair or at all the places at the table. Participants in ancient Greek and Roman banquets reclined while slaves stood throughout the meal. We therefore recline in yet another joyous recognition of freedom.

We begin the *seder* with candle lighting and the festival *Kiddush* over wine (see pages 142, 143). Then the *karpas*, or green vegetable, is dipped in salt water, mixing the promise of spring green with the salt of slavery's tears.

The Afikoman

The leader breaks the middle piece of matzah, setting one half aside for the *afikoman*. The *afikoman* is eaten at the end of the meal and no one can leave the *seder* without tasting it.

A marvelous custom has grown up around the *afikoman*. The *seder* leader hides it, and the children try to find it. Since the adults cannot finish their meal without the *afikoman*, they must then negotiate a settlement, usually a gift, to ensure its return.

Haggadah, matzah plate and cup for Elijah.

The Four Questions

The Four Questions (*Mah Nishtanah*) bring us to the heart of the Haggadah. How is this night different from all other nights? Traditionally, the Four Questions are asked by the youngest child able to ask them, or by all the children present (see page 146 to help your child practice):

> Why do we eat only matzah tonight?
>
> Why do we eat bitter herbs on Passover?
>
> Why do we dip twice?
>
> Why do we recline or lean back at the table?

Through these questions, the children are really asking for the reason we celebrate the Passover holiday. The Haggadah then gives us a set of answers.

Elijah's Cup

After the meal, we fill a cup of wine for Elijah the Prophet and open the door for his arrival. Tradition says that Elijah will return one day to announce the coming of the Messiah. Perhaps this year will at last bring the long-awaited message of redemption.

Passover for Children

In its most important aspects, Passover is for children. By explaining to them the rituals of Passover and by including them in our preparations—cleaning house, making *ḥaroset*, searching for *ḥametz*, setting out the *seder* plate—we help them

better understand the Passover *seder* itself and we prepare them to participate in it fully. In doing so, we endow them with the legacy of their heritage as Jews and fulfill God's commandment. "You shall tell your children on that day saying, 'It is because of what God did for me when I went free out of Egypt.' For God redeemed not only our ancestors, but us with them." (From the Haggadah)

Yom Ha-Shoah

Yom Ha-Shoah, literally "day of the calamity," commemorates the Holocaust. On this day we remember the six million Jews who perished and, in doing so, we confront head on questions about good and evil and God's role in the world.

............................▬............................

"Let there be abundant peace

from heaven . . ."

............................▬............................

FROM THE MOURNER'S KADDISH

In the Synagogue

Many newer prayer books contain rituals for Yom Ha-Shoah. Many synagogues hold special prayer services. Sometimes whole communities come together to remember, to memorialize, and to recite the Mourner's *Kaddish* for those who were killed.

Yom Ha-Shoah for Children

As parents, we try to shield our children from pain and from evil. But as Jews we also have the obligation to remember all the individuals whose lives were lost. Part of this obligation must include a retelling of the tragedy to our children. We must speak to them of a man named Hitler who, like Haman, wanted to kill all the Jews. This time, however, there was no Queen Esther to save them, and six million Jews were murdered.

Yom Ha-Atzma'ut

Some Jews have always lived in the Land of Israel. In the late 1800s others began returning to build new settlements there. This movement came partly in response to increasing anti-Semitism and escalating violence against Jews in Europe. However, the idea of reestablishing a Jewish state remained a radical and sometimes unpopular one for many years, even among Jews.

The publication of Theodore Herzl's tract *The Jewish State* in 1895 introduced the concept of political Zionism, and Herzl's efforts led to the convocation of a Jewish National Assembly and the establishment of the World Zionist Organization. Nevertheless, Herzl's dream of an internationally recognized, secure homeland for the Jewish people remained an elusive one for over half a century.

On the fifth of Iyar 5708, May 14, 1948, *Medinat Yisrael*, the State of Israel, was founded. The following day Israel was attacked by five Arab armies but emerged victorious, a new nation with its own language—modern Hebrew.

With the rebirth of the State of Israel, Judaism exists both in its homeland and in the Diaspora. Yom Ha-Atzma'ut, Independence Day, calls upon us to consider our relationship with Israel.

In Israel Yom Ha-Atzma'ut is preceded by Yom Ha-Zikaron, the day of remembering those who died while fighting for the state. The solemnity of this day, which includes lighting candles and reciting prayers for the dead, is followed by the exuberance of celebration on Israel's Independence Day.

In the Synagogue

The establishment of Yom Ha-Atzma'ut is so recent that the holiday lacks some of the ritualistic feel of other holidays. The Reform prayer book includes a service written especially for this day, and the Conservative prayer book contains a special prayer for the day.

Yom Ha-Atzma'ut for Children

For some children, connection with Israel takes the form only of an Israel bond purchased for them by Grandma and Grandpa when they were born. On Yom Ha-Atzma'ut, however, we can strengthen their attachment to Israel—and our own—by celebrating the founding of the Jewish state. In large cities the day is often marked by special parades. In many towns the Jewish community center and synagogues celebrate the day with Israeli music, films, dancing, and food. As part of the festivities, it is a wonderful time to learn the Israeli National Anthem, *Hatikvah*. Making paper flags to wave during the singing adds to the fun. And what better time to savor the taste of Israel by trying falafel (see page 163)!

Shavuot

Every year in late spring, Jews celebrate the giving of the Torah with the festival of Shavuot.

> When the people of Israel were gathered at the foot of Mount Sinai, God said to them, "What will you give Me as a surety pledge for the Torah?"
>
> The Israelites answered, "We will pledge all our gold and silver as surety for the Torah."
>
> But God did not accept this offer. "Even all the wealth in the world cannot measure up to this precious gift."
>
> The Israelites tried again: "We will pledge our ancestors as surety."
>
> "Your ancestors are in debt to Me," God replied. "How can they act as surety?"
>
> The Israelites thought for a long time. Finally they offered to God their most precious possessions.
>
> "We will pledge our children as surety for the Torah."
>
> "I accept your children as surety," God said. "For their sake you will observe the Law."

—From a midrash based on the Bible, written about 1,500 years ago

In biblical and Second Temple times, during the season of the Passover festival, farmers brought bundles of their first barley crop to Jerusalem. Waving these bundles, called *omer*, before the altar, they thanked God for a good start to the growing season. From the beginning of Passover, farmers counted forty-nine days more until the festival of first fruits," when they made another pilgrimage to Jerusalem, this time carrying bread loaves made from the summer's first wheat crop. The passing of forty-nine days, or seven weeks, lent the second festival its more familiar name, *Shavuot*, meaning "weeks." Shavuot always comes on the fiftieth day after the beginning of Passover.

In this original form, as a nature festival and pilgrimage, Shavuot could have lost much of its relevance when the Jews lost their Temple and their agricultural life on the land. But the Rabbis gave new meaning to Shavuot. After a thorough study of the Book of Exodus, they determined that the Israelites came to Mount Sinai seven weeks after they left Egypt. Therefore, they agreed, Shavuot's real function was the anniversary of the giving of the Torah. This inspired conclusion elevated Shavuot beyond its agricultural base. Now, every year in late spring, Jews celebrate the giving of the Torah with the festival of Shavuot.

At Sinai, God and the people of Israel entered into a covenant for all time. The Jews promised to observe God's Torah for themselves, their children, and every succeeding generation. Shavuot reminds us of that everlasting covenant and calls on us to look toward the future. We pledge ourselves not only to the distant memory of that epochal event at Sinai, but also to its faithful continuation.

Shavuot helps us to see ourselves as part of a long ladder reaching upward to Mount Sinai and to heaven. Legend has it that Moses climbed such a ladder to

Moses and Aaron with the text of the Ten Commandments.

Flemish painting, seventeenth century.

receive the Torah, which he then carried down to the people below. The Torah has since traveled, rung by rung, down the ladder of generations. Now it is our turn to take the heritage of our parents and grandparents and lovingly pass it on to our children.

Shavuot still speaks to us of nature. The world is never more luscious than at this time of year, somewhere between spring and summer, when the sights and smells of green, growing things fill the senses. Traditionally, Jews welcome Shavuot by decorating the synagogue with plants and flowers, making the indoor environment as pleasant as the outdoors.

At Home

Shavuot opens with the candle blessing, including the *Sheheḥeyanu, Kiddush,* and *Ha-Motzi* (see pages 142, 143). Then the festival meal is eaten.

A sixteenth-century rabbi, Moses Isserles, wrote, "It is a universal custom to eat dairy foods on the first day of Shavuot." Although we know that the eating of sweet foods made from milk is a very old Shavuot custom, we have no clear idea how it got started. A legend states that the people got so hungry while waiting for Moses to come down from the mountain that they fixed a quick meal from fresh milk. A Ḥasidic rabbi declared, "When the Jews received the Torah, they were considered as newborn infants who are only able to drink milk."

Yet another traditional explanation was that when the Israelites received the Torah, they realized that their cooking pots were not kosher and so ate a meal of cold dairy foods instead of cooking. Another plausible explanation lies in the biblical phrase "milk and honey," originally referring to the Land of Israel but later to Torah as well. We might say that the Torah tastes to us as delectable as a cheese blintz (see recipe page 164).

In the Synagogue

Throughout the generations, Jews have observed Shavuot with intense prayer and study. The sixteenth-century mystics spent the eve of Shavuot in the synagogue. All night long they studied the holy books, refreshing themselves with little cakes and an occasional sip of tea. They emerged at dawn and, squinting sleepy eyes at the sun, began a triumphant outdoor celebration of the festival service.

In our time Jews continue to view this holiday as an affirmation of Jewish study and education. On Shavuot many congregations hold Confirmation ceremonies, at which religious school students of high school age declare their readiness to join the adult Jewish community. Conservative synagogues often celebrate graduation exercises from religious school on Shavuot.

The scriptural reading for the Shavuot service includes a portion from the Book of Ruth. This book portrays Israel in the time of the Judges and contains one of the Bible's most moving passages.

Ruth declares her loyalty to her mother-in-law, Naomi, and promises to stay always by her side: *Entreat me not to leave thee and to return from following after thee; for wither thou goest, I will go; and where thou lodgest, I will lodge; thy people will be my people, and thy God my God.* (Ruth 1:16)

Shavuot for Children

In some parts of Eastern Europe, Shavuot was the time when children were introduced to Torah study. Parents would prepare a slate with the Hebrew letters of the *alef-bet* and cover it with honey. Following the first hesitant steps to learn Hebrew, the child would lick the slate; later the adults would offer cake. And so, it was said, Jewish children came to know the sweetness of Torah.

The Ten Commandments, or "The Ten Words," as they are actually called in Hebrew, constitute the core of the revelation at Sinai. From their first proclamation to a small group of fugitive ex-slaves in the wilderness, they have found their way into the laws of two other religious civilizations and to universal acceptance throughout the modern world.

You can carry on the Shavuot tradition of education and Torah by teaching your children about the Ten Commandments. They are found in the Book of Exodus beginning with chapter 20.

THE TEN COMMANDMENTS

1. *I am your God, who brought you out of the land of Egypt. Do not worship any other gods but Me.*
2. *Do not worship idols.*
3. *Do not take the name of your God in vain.*
4. *Remember the Sabbath day and keep it holy.*
5. *Honor your father and mother.*
6. *Do not murder.*
7. *Do not commit adultery.*
8. *Do not steal.*
9. *Do not bear false witness against your neighbor.*
10. *Do not covet.*

Shabbat

May God bless us with Shabbat joy.

May God bless us with Shabbat holiness.

May God bless us with Shabbat peace.

Our Weekly Holiday

We all work and we all need rest. Often, in building a better life for ourselves and our children, we leave little time unstructured—time just to be ourselves, time to be with family, time to appreciate our Jewishness. Even our moments of physical rest can fail to refresh us, because we do not put aside the pressures and anxieties of the everyday world.

Judaism urges us to set one day apart. On the seventh day, Shabbat, we concentrate on things that are different. From sundown on Friday night to Saturday evening we can appreciate the things that we are often too busy to notice during the week. We go to the synagogue, where we commemorate the work of our Creator and strengthen our ties with our Jewish community. We observe ceremonies that mark the uniqueness of the day. On Shabbat we enjoy family life, the foundation of all Jewish observance.

The original concept of Shabbat—a sanctified day of rest—is simple yet revolutionary, and writer after writer has added words of interpretation and acclaim. Shabbat is the only holiday to be included in the Ten Commandments. To our Rabbis, Shabbat represented the special relationship between God and the Jewish people. Medieval mystics described it as a union between the Shabbat "bride" and her happy "groom," the people of Israel. And a masterpiece of Jewish mystical literature, the *Zohar*, likened Shabbat to a taste of redemption, calling it "a mirror of the world to come."

While Jews throughout the ages have praised Shabbat as the most important holiday that kept the people together, many non-Jewish commentators have seen Shabbat as Judaism's most important gift to the rest of the world. Until the introduction of a day of rest, the great majority of humanity toiled from dawn to dusk, day after day and week after week. The renowned psychologist Erich Fromm hailed Shabbat as a one-day release from "the chains of time."

No single source can do justice to the meaning and importance of the Jewish Sabbath. We hope these fragments will encourage you to seek more information. Shabbat finds its most rewarding expression in the simple rituals followed at home. When you bring the fragrance of Shabbat into your family life, you bring yourself and your children closer to the very essence of Judaism.

Shabbat at Home

Friday evening dinner is the quintessential Shabbat experience. Many families share this time with grandparents or close friends. As the stillness of Sabbath peace, *Shabbat Shalom*, descends, we light at least two candles. Tradition ascribes each light to a different biblical reference: the Book of Exodus commands, "remember the Sabbath day" (20:8), while Deuteronomy says, "observe the Sabbath day" (5:12). Some people light a candle for each member of the family.

Then comes a very special moment—the blessing of the children. Through the gentle touch of your hands and the sound of your voice, your children will feel your love for them and your hopes for their future. This blessing is followed by the Shabbat *Kiddush* and *Ha-Motzi*, the blessing over the bread.

On Shabbat we eat a special bread called ḥallah. The Hebrew word *ḥallah* first appears in the Torah, where it means a portion of bread set aside for the priests. Unlike the dark bread eaten throughout the week, it was made from white flour and probably tasted sweet, like cake. Later the word came to mean the special braided bread Jews throughout the world eat on Shabbat.

Ḥallah also calls to mind manna, the food that God supplied to the Israelites during their forty years' wandering in the wilderness of Sinai. The Bible relates that the people were instructed to gather two portions of manna on Friday, one for that day and one for Shabbat. Jews still remember this double manna portion by placing two ḥallah loaves on the Shabbat table. The loaves are covered with a decorated cloth, reminiscent of the dew sent by God to keep the manna fresh overnight.

In the Synagogue

The mystics of the sixteenth-century Galilean community Ts'fat perceived Shabbat as a bride or queen. Every Friday evening, toward sunset, they gathered in the terraced fields outside the city and sang a welcoming greeting to their guest: "Come in peace . . . come in joy . . . come O bride, come!" Jews throughout the world still welcome the Sabbath with these words, which form part of the *L'khah Dodi* hymn sung at the beginning of the Friday evening service.

Since the time of the Bible, Judaism has established an increasingly elaborate set of restrictions and customs around Shabbat activity. All these rules have the same purpose—to emphasize the holiness of Shabbat by setting it apart from the other days of the week. The Jewish people have observed these laws and customs to enhance the enjoyment of Shabbat.

Attending synagogue services on Friday night or Saturday morning emphasizes the Shabbat difference. Here, through prayers, songs, and the reading of the weekly Torah portion, we celebrate the specialness of the Sabbath. Remembering that Shabbat is the day of rest, for the remainder of the day we seek relaxing pursuits that the whole family can share. Saturday afternoon is traditionally a time for a leisurely walk, visits with friends, and study.

Havdalah

So that the sweetness of Shabbat would last as long as possible, the Rabbis postponed its end until about an hour after sunset on Saturday. Before the era of clocks and watches, the stars were used to determine the end of Shabbat. When three stars are visible in the evening sky, it is time to bid farewell to Shabbat with the

Spices remind us of the sweetness of Shabbat.

Havdalah ("separation") ceremony.

A braided candle and a box filled with aromatic spices such as cloves or cinnamon are used during the ceremony. The traditional song *Eliyahu Ha-Navi* ("Elijah the Prophet") is sung at the conclusion. The Prophet Elijah is known throughout the Jewish world as the herald of redemption. We may not know when redemption will come, but we can accurately predict the arrival of the next best thing—Shabbat, a mere six days away.

A Home Shabbat Service

We welcome Shabbat simply. We light candles and recite a short blessing.
We recognize the importance of family in our lives by blessing our children.
We say a blessing over wine and over bread. We can add a song or two to the celebration. Shabbat has arrived!

If you are just beginning, do not feel you have to do it all. Start with lighting the candles. Add more as the blessings become more comfortable.

The Blessing of
the Candles.

*Painting by
Isidor Kaufman.
Vienna, nineteenth
century.*

Lighting the Shabbat Candles

Sabbath candles may be lit as early as 1 1/4 hours before sunset, but the usual time is up to 18 minutes before sunset. This is the procedure:

Light the candles.

Move your hands around the flames several times and bring them toward your face. This gesture symbolically welcomes the Sabbath into your home.

Place your hands over your eyes, so that you will not see the Sabbath lights until you have recited the blessing.

Barukh atah, Adonai Eloheinu,	בָּרוּךְ אַתָּה, יְיָ אֱלֹהֵינוּ,
melekh ha-olam,	מֶלֶךְ הָעוֹלָם,
asher kidshanu b'mitzvotav v'tzivanu	אֲשֶׁר קִדְּשָׁנוּ בְּמִצְוֹתָיו וְצִוָּנוּ
l'hadlik ner shel Shabbat.	לְהַדְלִיק נֵר שֶׁל שַׁבָּת.

*Blessed are You, Adonai our God, Ruler of the world, who makes us holy
with* mitzvot, *and commands us to kindle the Sabbath lights.*

Continue the home Shabbat service with the blessing for your children on the next page.

Blessing Your Children

Place your hands on your child's head and say the following:
For a daughter:

Y'simekh Elohim

k'sarah rivkah raḥel v'leah.

יְשִׂמֵךְ אֱלֹהִים
כְּשָׂרָה רִבְקָה רָחֵל וְלֵאָה.

May God make you like Sarah, Rebecca, Rachel, and Leah.

For a son:

Y'simkha Elohim

k'efrayim v'khimenasheh.

יְשִׂמְךָ אֱלֹהִים
כְּאֶפְרַיִם וְכִמְנַשֶּׁה.

May God make you like Ephraim and Menasseh.

The blessing continues for all children:

Y'varekh'kha Adonai v'yishm'rekha.
Ya'er Adonai panav elekha viḥuneka.
Yisa Adonai panav elekha, v'yasem
l'kha shalom.

יְבָרֶכְךָ יְיָ וְיִשְׁמְרֶךָ.
יָאֵר יְיָ פָּנָיו אֵלֶיךָ וִיחֻנֶּךָּ.
יִשָּׂא יְיָ פָּנָיו אֵלֶיךָ וְיָשֵׂם
לְךָ שָׁלוֹם.

May God Bless you and keep you.
May God's light shine on you and be gracious to you.
May God's face be lifted upon you and give you peace.

Continue the home Shabbat service with the *Kiddush*, the blessing over the wine.

Kiddush for Shabbat

(Blessing over the Wine)

Hold the wine cup in your right hand as you recite the blessings:

Barukh atah, Adonai Eloheinu,

melekh ha-olam,

borei pri ha-gafen.

בָּרוּךְ אַתָּה, יְיָ אֱלֹהֵינוּ,
מֶלֶךְ הָעוֹלָם,
בּוֹרֵא פְּרִי הַגָּפֶן.

Blessed are You, Adonai our God, Ruler of the world, who creates the fruit of the vine.

For those who are more fluent in Hebrew, there is a longer version of Kiddush:

בָּרוּךְ אַתָּה, יְיָ אֱלֹהֵינוּ, מֶלֶךְ הָעוֹלָם, בּוֹרֵא פְּרִי הַגָּפֶן.
בָּרוּךְ אַתָּה, יְיָ אֱלֹהֵינוּ, מֶלֶךְ הָעוֹלָם, אֲשֶׁר קִדְּשָׁנוּ
בְּמִצְוֹתָיו וְרָצָה בָנוּ, וְשַׁבַּת קָדְשׁוֹ בְּאַהֲבָה וּבְרָצוֹן
הִנְחִילָנוּ, זִכָּרוֹן לְמַעֲשֵׂה בְרֵאשִׁית. כִּי הוּא יוֹם תְּחִלָּה
לְמִקְרָאֵי קֹדֶשׁ, זֵכֶר לִיצִיאַת מִצְרָיִם. כִּי בָנוּ בָחַרְתָּ
וְאוֹתָנוּ קִדַּשְׁתָּ מִכָּל הָעַמִּים, וְשַׁבַּת קָדְשְׁךָ בְּאַהֲבָה
וּבְרָצוֹן הִנְחַלְתָּנוּ. בָּרוּךְ אַתָּה יְיָ, מְקַדֵּשׁ הַשַּׁבָּת.

Barukh atah, Adonai Eloheinu, melekh ha-olam, borei pri ha-gafen.
Barukh atah, Adonai Eloheinu, melekh ha-olam, asher kidshanu
bemitzvotav veratzah vanu, v'shabbat kodsho be'ahavah uveratzon
hinḥilanu, zikaron lema'aseh vereishit. Ki hu yom teḥilah
lemikra'ei kodesh, zekher litziyat Mitzrayim. Ki vanu vaḥarta
ve'otanu kidashta mikol ha-amim, v'shabbat kod'shekha Be'ahava
uveratzon hinḥaltanu. Barukh atah Adonai, mekadesh ha-shabbat.

Blessed are You, Adonai our God, Ruler of the world, who creates the fruit of the vine.

Blessed are You, Adonai our God, Ruler of the world, who makes us holy with commandments and takes delight in us. In God's love and favor God has made the holy Sabbath our heritage, as a memory of the work of creation.

It is the first among holy days, a memory of the going out from Egypt. You chose us from all the nations and You made us holy, and in love and favor You have given us the Sabbath as a sacred inheritance. Praised are You, Adonai, who makes the Sabbath holy.

Continue the home Shabbat service with *Ha-Motzi*

Ha-Motzi

(Blessing over the Bread)

Barukh atah, Adonai Eloheinu,

melekh ha-olam,

ha-motzi leḥem min ha-aretz.

בָּרוּךְ אַתָּה, יְיָ אֱלֹהֵינוּ,
מֶלֶךְ הָעוֹלָם,
הַמּוֹצִיא לֶחֶם מִן הָאָרֶץ.

*Blessed are You, Adonai our God, Ruler of the world,
who brings forth bread from the earth.*

Shalom Aleikhem

This traditional song calls forth the peace of Shabbat.

*Peace unto you,
Oh Angels of peace;
May your coming
and going
be in peace.*

Havdalah Service

Traditionally, Shabbat ends when three stars can be seen in the sky. The sun has set, we recite the blessing over the wine, we pass around the spice box to savor that last moment of our sweet day, and finally, in the glow of the *Havdalah* candle, we recite the blessing of separation that sets Shabbat apart from the rest of our week.

Kiddush

Again we say the blessing over the wine.

Fill the wine cup to overflowing, allowing some of the wine to spill onto the plate. Lift the cup and recite the short version of the *Kiddush*.

Barukh atah, Adonai Eloheinu,

melekh ha-olam,

borei pri ha-gafen.

בָּרוּךְ אַתָּה, יְיָ אֱלֹהֵינוּ,
מֶלֶךְ הָעוֹלָם,
בּוֹרֵא פְּרִי הַגָּפֶן.

Blessed are You, Adonai Our God, Ruler of the world, who creates the fruit of the vine.

Set the cup down and continue with the blessing over the spices below.

Blessing over the Aromatic Spices

Barukh atah, Adonai Eloheinu,

melekh ha-olam,

borei minay v'samim.

בָּרוּךְ אַתָּה, יְיָ אֱלֹהֵינוּ,
מֶלֶךְ הָעוֹלָם,
בּוֹרֵא מִינֵי בְשָׂמִים.

Blessed are You, Adonai our God, Ruler of the world, who creates all kinds of spices.

Life the spice holder.

Sniff the spices, then pass the spice box around to allow each person to smell them.

Continue with the blessing over the *Havdalah* candle, next page.

Blessing over the Havdalah Candle

Then continue with the following blessing:

Barukh atah, Adonai Eloheinu,

melekh ha-olam,

borei m'oray ha-esh.

בָּרוּךְ אַתָּה, יְיָ אֱלֹהֵינוּ,
מֶלֶךְ הָעוֹלָם,
בּוֹרֵא מְאוֹרֵי הָאֵשׁ.

Blessed are You, Adonai our God, Ruler of the world, who creates the lights.

Next, light the candle, hold it in your right hand, and recite the final prayer, which speaks of *Havdalah*, separation. The twilight hour has passed. We have crossed the line dividing Shabbat from the rest of the week.

Those who are more fluent in Hebrew may recite a longer version:

Barukh atah, Adonai Eloheinu,

melekh ha-olam,

ha-mavdeel bein kodesh l'hol.

בָּרוּךְ אַתָּה, יְיָ אֱלֹהֵינוּ,
מֶלֶךְ הָעוֹלָם,
הַמַּבְדִּיל בֵּין-קֹדֶשׁ לְחֹל.

Blessed are You, Adonai, who makes a distinction between sacred and secular.

Everyone who wants to takes a sip from the cup. Then extinguish the candle in the wine that is on the plate.

Eliyahu Ha-Navi

Finally, Elijah the Prophet is remembered, for he has traditionally symbolized our hope for the messianic age.

May the prophet Elijah come soon, in our time,
with the Messiah, son of David.

3

The Rhythm of Our Homes:

A Guide to Home Observance

SYMBOLS OF A JEWISH HOME

HOLIDAY BLESSINGS, RITUALS, AND SONGS

THE RHYTHM OF THE KITCHEN

Symbols of a Jewish Home

"Inscribe them on the doorposts

of your house, and on your gates."

—

DEUTERONOMY 6:9

Ritual Objects for the Jewish Home

Walking to the beat of a different drummer. This is the feeling we sometimes experience in trying to live a Jewish life in the midst of a modern world that has other priorities, other holidays, even another calendar. But when the surrounding culture cannot provide us with our Judaism, we must depend upon ourselves, creating it in our homes by surrounding ourselves with talismans that will transport us to our Judaism each time we enter, each time we mark a holiday or welcome Shabbat. By helping us celebrate the Jewish events of our lives, ritual objects mark our homes as special places where Judaism thrives.

The following list is neither comprehensive nor compulsory. It is merely a guide to a few of the basic ritual objects that will help you observe Shabbat and the holidays with a feeling of specialness and celebration. They can be items (such as candlesticks) that you already have but may want to designate for holiday or Shabbat use only; they can also be something purchased specially for their purpose, or even made. Many ritual objects make excellent craft projects for children.

Shabbat Candlesticks

The warmth and peace of the weekly holiday descends as the Shabbat lights are kindled on Friday evening. The simple gesture of lighting candles separates this time from the rest of the week, reminding us to hold Shabbat special and apart from the everyday demands we all face.

Traditionally, Shabbat candles are lit by the women of the household. As night falls, the match is struck. Hands circle the lighted candles, then cover the eyes as the blessing is recited. This custom arises from the traditional prohibition against lighting fire on Shabbat. Normally a blessing is offered before a ritual takes place (we bless the wine, then drink it, for example). However, because Shabbat begins when we say the blessing, tradition requires the lights to be kindled before the blessing. By covering our eyes, we help preserve the notion that the lights are not really lit until the blessing has been offered. We open our eyes to the light of the candles: Shabbat has begun.

Shabbat candlesticks can be of any type or style. There should be at least two, but some families have one for each family member. Usually Shabbat candlesticks are reserved solely for Shabbat and holiday use; they would not be used as all-purpose table ornaments. Candles (usually white) of any sort may be used, but many people prefer the white, 4-inch paraffin Shabbat candles sold in many grocery stores. Shabbat candles should be long enough to burn throughout the Friday night dinner. They are never extinguished but are allowed to burn themselves out completely. The blessing over the candles can be found on page 125 for Shabbat and on page 142 for other holidays.

Kiddush *Cups*

We acknowledge the special sanctity of Shabbat by blessing a cup of wine. As we lift the cup, we recite the *Kiddush*, praising God, creator of the fruit of the vine. Traditionally, it is the father who recites the blessing, although many families say the blessing together. While only one cup is needed to perform this ritual, having a special *Kiddush* cup for each family member enhances the Shabbat celebration.

Kiddush cups are used year round at Shabbat, as well as for the blessing over the wine during holiday festivals, and they can be used during the Passover *seder* as well. Like Shabbat candlesticks, *Kiddish* cups are usually reserved for their special purpose and are not used for everyday drinking. Children can make their own, using plastic wine glasses dec-orated with colored tissue paper, stickers, and other

Kiddush cup for Shavuot.
Made by Georg Nicolaus Bierfreund

decorative items. Silver *Kiddush* cups make especially beautiful wedding and baby gifts. Don't forget a separate *Kiddush* cup for Elijah at the Passover table. The blessing over the wine on Shabbat can be found on page 127. The *Kiddush* for other holidays is on page 143.

Ḥallah *Cover*

It is said that the bread should not be made to feel slighted because the blessing over the wine comes first. Thus, we cover the ḥallah during the candle lighting and the *Kiddush*. A simple napkin will suffice, but a special cloth, perhaps embroidered or decorated with fabric paints, makes a beautiful addition to the Shabbat table.

At the proper moment, with the candles burning and the *Kiddush* completed, the ḥallah cover is removed and the blessing over the bread is recited. Then each person present takes and eats a small piece of the bread. The *Ha-Motzi*, the bless-ing over the bread, can be found on page 128.

Spice *Box*

Saying goodbye to Shabbat in the beautiful *Havdalah* ceremony is a very special way to separate this day from the rest of the week. We savor the fragrance of the sweet spices at the end of Shabbat in the hope that the sweetness of the day can be with us through the coming week.

Of course, the blessing over the spices can be said using the jar of cinnamon taken directly from the kitchen cabinet. However, a special box—whether a small film can-

Silver spice box.

Frankfort-am-Main, ca. 1550

ister embellished by a child with glitter and stickers; an ornate, silver antique; or something in between—can add both to our enjoyment of this special ritual and to the spirit of Judaism in our home. The blessing over aromatic spices can be found on page 129.

Havdalah *Candle*

This special candle, to be burned at the end of Shabbat, is distinguished by its intricate braids and many wicks. As Shabbat draws to a close, wine is poured into the *Kiddush* cup until it overflows into a saucer set below it. The candle, usually held by a child, is lit. The *Kiddush* over wine is recited, as well as the blessing over the spices. After the spice box is passed to all present, the blessing over the candle is recited, and its flame is extinguished in the spilled wine. Shabbat is over until the next week.

Judaica stores and temple gift shops are excellent sources for *Havdalah* candles. They also make lovely mementos to bring home from your travels. The blessing over the *Havdalah* candle is found on page 130.

Tzedakah *Box*

Charitable giving is such an important part of so many Jewish holidays and events that it comes as no surprise that the *tzedakah* box is an enduring feature of the Jewish home. It, like many ritual objects, can take many forms, either crafted by young hands or created by skilled artisans, or even given out by one of the many Jewish relief organizations. Whatever its provenance, the importance of the box derives from its use in collecting our contributions to fulfill our obligation to help others.

It is the custom to give *tzedakah* at Shabbat and on many holidays, as well as in celebration of personal milestones such as birthdays and Bar/Bat Mitzvah, and to honor the memory of loved ones.

Ḥanukkiah

The winter days are dark, night coming ever earlier as the shortest day of the year approaches. Against this darkness, the growing glow of the *Ḥanukkah* lights can seem especially heartening as we are reminded not only of ancient miracles, but of the spring that will be coming as the days begin to lengthen again. It is Ḥanukkah, a time of joy, a celebration of freedom and of light.

What better way to celebrate than through the lighting of candles on the *ḥanukkiah*? This special candelabra, also called a Ḥanukkah menorah, has nine branches: one for each of the eight nights of Ḥanukkah, plus a ninth spot for the "helper" candle, or *shamash*, used to light the others. Other than the number of branches, the only requirement for a *ḥanukkiah* is that one branch be placed at a different level (either higher or lower) than the other eight. Ḥanukkah candles can be of any type, as long as they will burn for at least half an hour.

Although only one *ḥanukkiah* is needed to kindle the Ḥanukkah lights, many families collect them over the years, the first one being joined later by religious school creations, baby gifts, Bar and Bat Mitzvah presents, etc. Once the fun starts, everyone in the family may want his or her own! Since they are easy to make, easy to find, beautiful in every window that will accommodate one, you may find the *ḥanukkiyot* in your home multiplying faster than markers in a good game of *dreidel*. The blessing for the kindling of Ḥanukkah lights is on page 146.

Seder *Plate*

We gather around the Passover table each year to tell and retell the story of our ancestors and their escape from Egypt. We are commanded to remember and to regard ourselves as having been personally freed from Egypt. To aid in our remembrance and our retelling, we bring special symbols—ritual foods—to the Passover table, to act as visual aids in the annual drama of the Passover *seder*.

These foods are placed on a special plate, set out in a prescribed order. Proceeding clockwise around the plate, they are: *zeroah*, זְרוֹעַ, a roasted lamb bone; *ḥaroset*, חֲרוֹסֶת, a mixture of nuts, apples, and wine; *karpas*, כַּרְפַּס, green vegetable (lettuce and/or parsley); *betzah*, בֵּיצָה, roasted egg; and *maror*, מָרוֹר, bitter herbs (traditionally, horseradish).

Seder plates may be made of any material. Some have indentations to accommodate each of the ritual foods. Typically they are decorated with words or pictures to indicate which food goes where on the plate. *Seder* plates make a wonderful craft for children; a paper or plastic plate can be decorated with crayons and markers.

Yahrzeit *Candles*

Yahrzeit is a Yiddish word meaning "anniversary." To honor the memory of a loved one, especially a parent, we light a *yahrzeit* candle on the Hebrew date of death. The candle should burn 24 hours, from sundown to sundown, and the Mourner's *Kaddish* is recited. According to tradition, only children are required to say *Kaddish* for a parent. Although we may also recite it for others, doing so is not considered an obligation.

Yahrzeit is also a time to visit the graves of loved ones, to offer *tzedakah* in their honor, and to attend Shabbat services. In the synagogue, names of the departed are read on their *yahrzeit*.

Yahrzeit candles are simple: plain glass jars filled with wax. They are available in many grocery stores and through your synagogue. In recent years special yellow *yahrzeit* candles have come into use for remembrance at Yom Hashoah. The Mourner's *Kaddish* can be found on page 85.

Mezuzah

Jewish homes are dedicated by the affixing of a *mezuzah* to the doorposts of the house. The *mezuzah* consists of a container made of wood, metal, stone, or ceramic containing a parchment scroll. Two passages from the Torah are lettered on the front of the scroll (Deuteronomy 6:4–9 and 11:13–21). The word *Shaddai* (Almighty) is lettered on the back. Usually this word can be seen through a hole in the container. Otherwise the container often has the word or the Hebrew letter *shin* displayed on its front.

The *mezuzah* is affixed on the right-hand side as one enters. It is attached within the upper third of the doorpost. It is fastened diagonally, the top slanted toward the house. Before affixing the *mezuzah*, say this blessing:

Barukh atah, Adonai Eloheinu, melekh ha-olam, asher kid-shanu b'mitzvotav v'tzivanu likboah mezuzah.

Praised are You, Adonai our God, Ruler of the world, who makes us holy with mitzvot and commands us to affix the mezuzah.

"Blessed are You,

Adonai our God, Ruler of the world,

who makes us holy with commandments

and commands us to kindle the festival lights."

BLESSING OVER THE
FESTIVAL CANDLES

Celebrating Our Festivals

Our annual cycle of holidays has its roots in both ancient and modern times, and the origin of each helps determine how it is celebrated. Some holidays, like Shabbat, Rosh Hashanah, and Yom Kippur, are biblically ordained, while others, such as Ḥanukkah and Purim, are considered rabbinic holidays, marking ancient miracles. Still others, notably Yom Hashoah and Yom Ha-Atzma'ut, are special days set aside during the modern era to mark events that have happened in our own time.

Our biblical holidays are considered *mikra'ei kodesh*, days of holy assembly, and are marked by the basic home festival service, which includes lighting candles, saying the *Kiddush* over wine, and reciting *Ha-Motzi* over bread. A *Havdalah* service at the close of each festival would also be considered appropriate, although this is a custom followed primarily by traditional Jews. Traditional Jews also observe the prohibition against work on these festival days (although cooking is allowed). The *mikra'ei kodesh* are Rosh Hashanah, Yom Kippur, the first and last days of Sukkot, and the first and last days of Passover.

Some Jews observe these holidays for two days. This custom was devised to accommodate Jews of the Diaspora, who might not be able to discern with accuracy when a particular holiday had begun. Since the Jewish calendar is a lunar one, the first day of each month falls at the new moon, which can be one of two days each lunar cycle. Although the two-day holiday has been discontinued by many (and is not practiced in Israel), many traditional Jews have maintained it. Yom Kippur, however, is kept to only one day, because the rabbis viewed fasting for 48 hours too harsh.

Other holidays, notably Purim and Ḥanukkah, have special customs but are typically not celebrated with a full home service. Purim is generally marked by participation in reading aloud of the *Megillat Esther*, and Ḥanukkah, of course, means lighting the Ḥanukkah candles! In recent years Yom Hashoah and Yom Ha-Atzma'ut have been marked by special synagogue services, but there is usually no home service.

On the following pages you will find some of our most basic home rituals. The blessings and prayers are given in both English and Hebrew, along with a Hebrew transliteration. They will help start you on your way.

When you recite the blessings, try to follow the Hebrew form as it has been handed down for generations. If you cannot read Hebrew, you can use the transliteration provided along with each Hebrew text. You and your family will find comfort in repeating the same structure again and again, holiday after holiday, year after year. You will hear mystery in the words and beauty in the old melodies. The blessings will become familiar, and soon you and your children will know the ceremonies by heart, without having consciously tried to memorize them. When you read prayers and blessings in English, you help your children to understand the meanings of the blessings you say together.

Feel free to pick and choose the parts of the various holiday services you wish to use, the ones you feel more comfortable with, the ones you and your family like the most. You may wish to begin by trying one ritual, such as lighting candles, and then add others over time. In this way your celebration of the holidays can grow as your children grow, and you truly make the traditions your own.

The Jewish home is referred to as a *mikdash me'at*, a miniature sanctuary. A sanctuary or shelter is marked by tranquility and holiness. The kind of sanctuary you build together depends on the choices you make. When you bring Jewish rituals into your home, you bring with them the values and customs that have helped the Jewish family and the Jewish people to endure. For a guide to the secular dates of Jewish holidays, consult the table on page 152.

Blessings for Festivals

The home services for holidays are simple and straightforward. We light candles and say a blessing over them; we express our happiness at having come to this special time; we recite a blessing over wine and one over bread. The holiday has begun.

On some holidays there are other blessings that can be added: at Sukkot we can recite blessings for the *sukkah* and for the *lulav* and *etrog*; at Ḥanukkah we can acknowledge the miracles performed on our behalf so long ago. Before the start of Passover we can search for forbidden leaven (*ḥametz*) and declare any undiscovered *ḥametz* nonexistent, thus ritually cleansing our homes for the festival. During the *seder* a child, usually the youngest who is able, recites the Four Questions.

Candle Lighting for Festivals

The following blessing is said on the eve of all festivals except Yom Kippur. The candles are lit just before sunset. When the festival occurs on Shabbat, add the words in brackets.

Barukh atah, Adonai Eloheinu,

melekh ha-olam,

asher kidshanu b'mitzvotav

v'tzivanu l'hadleek ner

shel [Shabbat v'] yom tov.

בָּרוּךְ אַתָּה יְיָ, אֱלֹהֵינוּ,

מֶלֶךְ הָעוֹלָם,

אֲשֶׁר קִדְּשָׁנוּ בְּמִצְוֹתָיו

וְצִוָּנוּ לְהַדְלִיק נֵר

שֶׁל (שַׁבָּת וְ) יוֹם טוֹב.

Blessed are You, Adonai our God, Ruler of the world, who makes us holy with mitzvot, and commands us to kindle the [Sabbath and the] festival lights.

On the first eve of the festival, continue with the Sheheḥeyanu:

Barukh atah, Adonai Eloheinu,

melekh ha-olam,

sheheḥeyanu v'kiyemanu

v'higiyanu lazman ha-zeh.

בָּרוּךְ אַתָּה יְיָ, אֱלֹהֵינוּ,

מֶלֶךְ הָעוֹלָם,

שֶׁהֶחֱיָנוּ וְקִיְּמָנוּ

וְהִגִּיעָנוּ לַזְּמַן הַזֶּה.

Blessed are You, Adonai our God, Ruler of the world, who has given us life, sustained us, and brought us to this season of joy.

Candle Lighting for Yom Kippur

Candles are lit just before sunset on the eve of Yom Kippur. When Yom Kippur occurs on Shabbat, add the words in brackets.

Barukh atah, Adonai Eloheinu,

melekh ha-olam,

asher kidshanu b'mitzvotav

v'tzivanu l'hadleek ner

shel [Shabbat v'] yom ha-kippurim.

בָּרוּךְ אַתָּה יְיָ, אֱלֹהֵינוּ,

מֶלֶךְ הָעוֹלָם,

אֲשֶׁר קִדְּשָׁנוּ בְּמִצְוֹתָיו

וְצִוָּנוּ לְהַדְלִיק נֵר

שֶׁל (שַׁבָּת וְ) יוֹם הַכִּפּוּרִים.

Blessed are You, Adonai our God, Ruler of the world, who makes us holy with mitzvot, and commands us to kindle the [Sabbath and the] Yom Kippur lights.

Continue with the *Sheheḥeyanu* (see above).

Kiddush *for Festivals*

Take the wine cup in your right hand as you recite the blessing.

Barukh atah, Adonai Eloheinu,

melekh ha-olam

borei p'ree ha-gafen.

בָּרוּךְ אַתָּה, יְיָ אֱלֹהֵינוּ,
מֶלֶךְ הָעוֹלָם,
בּוֹרֵא פְּרִי הַגָּפֶן.

Blessed are You, Adonai our God, Ruler of the world, creator of the fruit of the vine.

Drink the wine. Then complete the festival home service with *Ha-Motzi.*

Ha-Motzi *for Festivals*

Before eating on the festival day, remove the cover from the bread and recite the blessing.
Eat the bread.

Barukh atah, Adonai Eloheinu,

melekh ha-olam,

ha-motzi leḥem min ha-aretz.

בָּרוּךְ אַתָּה, יְיָ אֱלֹהֵינוּ,
מֶלֶךְ הָעוֹלָם,
הַמּוֹצִיא לֶחֶם מִן הָאָרֶץ.

Blessed are You, Adonai our God, Ruler of the world,
who brings forth bread from the earth.

Special Holiday Blessings and Songs

In addition to the basic elements of the home festival service, some holidays include rituals relating specifically to that special day. Some of these blessings, songs, and prayers are provided on the following pages.

Sukkot: Blessing for the Sukkah

Barukh atah, Adonai Eloheinu,

melekh ha-olam,

asher kidshanu b'mitzvotav

v'tzivanu leishev ba-sukkah.

בָּרוּךְ אַתָּה, יְיָ אֱלֹהֵינוּ,

מֶלֶךְ הָעוֹלָם,

אֲשֶׁר קִדְּשָׁנוּ בְּמִצְוֹתָיו

וְצִוָּנוּ לֵישֵׁב בַּסֻּכָּה.

Blessed are You, Adonai our God, Ruler of the world, who makes us holy with mitzvot, *and commands us to sit in the* sukkah.

Sukkot: Blessing over the Lulav and Etrog

This blessing can be recited at home in the *sukkah*. Traditional Jews perform this ritual each day during Sukkot, except on Shabbat.

Hold the *etrog* in your left hand, the *lulav* in your right.

Barukh atah, Adonai Eloheinu,

melekh ha-olam,

asher kidshanu b'mitzvotav

v'tzivanu al n'teelat lulav.

בָּרוּךְ אַתָּה, יְיָ אֱלֹהֵינוּ,

מֶלֶךְ הָעוֹלָם,

אֲשֶׁר קִדְּשָׁנוּ בְּמִצְוֹתָיו

וְצִוָּנוּ עַל־נְטִילַת לוּלָב.

Blessed are You, Adonai our God, Ruler of the world, who makes us holy with mitzvot and commands us concerning the waving of the palm branch.

Tu B'Shevat: Blessing over the Fruits

At a Tu B'Shevat *seder* we celebrate the earth and its bounty by drinking four different cups of wine and by sampling many different kinds of fruit and nuts. Try to taste some from each of three different categories: (1) those with peels or shells that are not eaten (most nuts, oranges, bananas, melons); (2) those with pits that are not eaten (cherries, dates, prunes and plums, olives, apricots); and (3) those that can be completely consumed (seedless grapes, strawberries, pears, raisins, apples, figs). The following blessing is recited over the fruit:

Barukh atah, Adonai Eloheinu,

melekh ha-olam,

borei p'ree ha-etz.

בָּרוּךְ אַתָּה יְיָ, אֱלֹהֵינוּ,
מֶלֶךְ הָעוֹלָם,
בּוֹרֵא פְּרִי הָעֵץ.

Blessed are You, Adonai our God, Ruler of the world, creator of the fruit of the tree.

Ḥanukkah: Blessing over the Ḥanukkah Candles

There is no prescribed time to light Ḥanukkah candles. You may do so at sunset, or you may wait until well after dark, to allow the full beauty of the candlelight to be enjoyed. The *Ḥanukkiah* is usually placed in a window. As you face the Ḥanukkah *menorah*, place the first candle on your right. Subsequent candles are added to the left of it. The newest candles are always lit first, so you add candles from right to left but light them from left to right.

Light the *shamash*, take it in your hand, and say the following two blessings.

Barukh atah, Adonai Eloheinu,	בָּרוּךְ אַתָּה, יְיָ אֱלֹהֵינוּ,
melekh ha-olam,	מֶלֶךְ הָעוֹלָם,
asher kidshanu b'mitzvotav	אֲשֶׁר קִדְּשָׁנוּ בְּמִצְוֹתָיו
v'tzivanu l'hadleek ner	וְצִוָּנוּ לְהַדְלִיק נֵר
shel ḥanukkah.	שֶׁל חֲנֻכָּה.

Blessed are You, Adonai our God, Ruler of the world, who makes us holy with mitzvot and commands us to kindle the Ḥanukkah lights.

Barukh atah, Adonai Eloheinu,	בָּרוּךְ אַתָּה, יְיָ אֱלֹהֵינוּ,
melekh ha-olam,	מֶלֶךְ הָעוֹלָם,
she'asah nisim la-avoteinu	שֶׁעָשָׂה נִסִּים לַאֲבוֹתֵינוּ
ba-yameem ha-hem ba-zman ha-zeh.	בַּיָּמִים הָהֵם בַּזְּמַן הַזֶּה.

Blessed are You, Adonai our God, Ruler of the world, who did wondrous things for our people long ago at this time of year.

On the first night of Ḥanukkah only, add the *Sheheḥeyanu* blessing:

Barukh atah Adonai, Eloheinu,	בָּרוּךְ אַתָּה יְיָ, אֱלֹהֵינוּ,
melekh ha-olam,	מֶלֶךְ הָעוֹלָם,
sheheḥeyanu v'kiyemanu v'higiyanu	שֶׁהֶחֱיָנוּ וְקִיְּמָנוּ וְהִגִּיעָנוּ
la-zman ha-zeh.	לַזְּמַן הַזֶּה.

Blessed are You, Adonai our God, Ruler of the world, who has given us life, sustained us, and brought us to this season of joy.

Ḥanukkah: Maoz Tzur (Rock of Ages)

This song is traditionally sung right after the Ḥanukkah candles are lit.

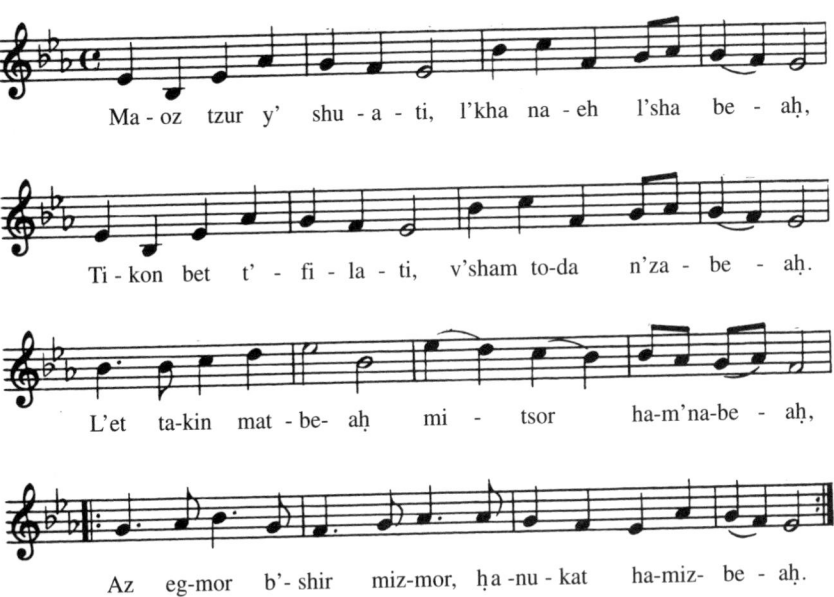

Ma - oz tzur y' shu - a - ti, l'kha na - eh l'sha be - aḥ,

Ti - kon bet t' - fi - la - ti, v'sham to-da n'za - be - aḥ.

L'et ta-kin mat - be- aḥ mi - tsor ha-m'na-be - aḥ,

Az eg-mor b'- shir miz-mor, ḥa -nu - kat ha-miz- be - aḥ.

Rock of Ages, let our song praise Your saving power;
You, amid the raging foes, were our sheltering tower.
Furious, they assailed us, but Your arm availed us,
And Your word broke their sword, when our own strength failed us.

Passover: Mah Nishtanah—The Four Questions

מַה נִּשְׁתַּנָּה הַלַּיְלָה הַזֶּה מִכָּל הַלֵּילוֹת.
שֶׁבְּכָל הַלֵּילוֹת אָנוּ אוֹכְלִין חָמֵץ וּמַצָּה,
הַלַּיְלָה הַזֶּה כֻּלּוֹ מַצָּה.

Mah nishtanah halaylah hazeh mikol halaylot!
Shebekol halaylot ahnu okhlin hametz u 'matzah;
Halayla hazeh kulo matzah?

How different this night is from all other nights!
On all other nights, we eat either bread or matzah; why tonight only matzah?

שֶׁבְּכָל הַלֵּילוֹת אָנוּ אוֹכְלִין שְׁאָר יְרָקוֹת,
הַלַּיְלָה הַזֶּה מָרוֹר.

Shebekol halaylot ahnu okhlin sh'ahr y'rahkot;
Halaylah hazeh maror?

On all other nights, we eat all kinds of vegetables; why tonight bitter herbs?

שֶׁבְּכָל הַלֵּילוֹת אֵין אָנוּ מַטְבִּילִין אֲפִלּוּ פַּעַם אֶחָת,
הַלַּיְלָה הַזֶּה שְׁתֵּי פְעָמִים.

Shebekol halaylot ayn ahnu okhlin matbilin afilu pa'ahm ehhat;
Halaylah hazeh shtay f'ahmim?

On all other nights, we do not dip our vegetables at all;
why tonight do we dip them twice?

שֶׁבְּכָל הַלֵּילוֹת אָנוּ אוֹכְלִין בֵּין יוֹשְׁבִין וּבֵין מְסֻבִּין,
הַלַּיְלָה הַזֶּה כֻּלָּנוּ מְסֻבִּין.

Shebekol halaylot ahnu okhlin bayn yoshvin u'vayn m'subin;
Halaylah hazeh kulanu m'subin?

On all other nights, we eat either sitting up or reclining;
Why tonight do we all recline?

Mah Nishtanah

Hagada   *Israeli*

Ma nish-ta-na ha-lai-la ha-ze mi kol __ ha-lë-lot, mi-

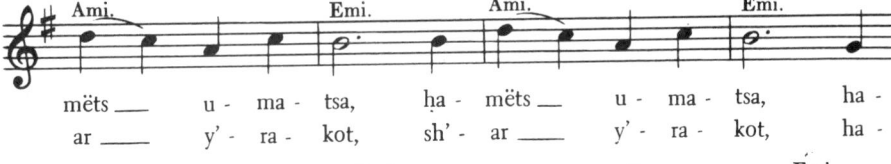

kol ha-lë-lot? 1. She-b'-ḥol ha-lë-lot a-nu oḥ-lin ḥa-
           ḥol ha-lë-lot a-nu oḥ-lin sh'-

mëts __ u-ma-tsa, ḥa-mëts __ u-ma-tsa, ha-
ar __ y'-ra-kot, sh'-ar __ y'-ra-kot, ha-

lai-la ha-ze, ha-lai-la ha-ze ku-lo __ ma-tsa, ha-
lai-la ha-ze, ha-lai-la ha-ze ku-lo __ ma-ror, ha-

lai-la ha-ze, ha-lai-la ha-ze ku __ lo ma-tsa. 2.She-b'-
lai-la ha-ze, ha-lai-la ha-ze ku __ lo ma-ror.

Passover: Dayenu — A Song of Gratitude

Hagada

Folk song

Rhythmically

SOLO:

I - lu ho - tsi, ho - tsi - o - nu, ho - tsi - o - nu mi-Mits - ra - yim,

ho - tsi - o - nu mi - Mits - ra - yim, da - yë - nu.

I - lu ho - tsi, ho - tsi - o - nu, ho - tsi - o - nu mi - Mits - ra - yim,

CHORUS:

ho - tsi - o - nu mi-Mits - ra - yim, da - yë - nu. Da - da - yë - nu,___

da - da - yë- nu,___ da - da-yë - nu, da - yë-nu, da- yë-nu, - - yë- nu, da - yë - nu.

Ilu no-san lo-nu et ha-Shabbat, dayenu.

Ilu no-san lo nu et ha-Torah, dayenu.

Ilu hih-ni-so-nu l'erets Yisroel, dayenu.

> Had God done nothing more than take us out of Egypt, dayenu
> (for that alone we should have been grateful).
> Had God given us Shabbat and nothing more, dayenu.
> Had God given us the Torah and nothing more, dayenu.
> Had God brought us into the land of Israel, dayenu.

Passover: The Search for Leaven

The search for leaven (*Bedikat Ḥametz*) takes place on the night before the first Passover *seder*. When the first evening of Passover falls on Saturday night, this ritual is conducted on Thursday. You will need a feather, a wooden spoon, and a paper bag. To begin, with the house dark, light the candle and say this blessing:

Barukh atah, Adonai Eloheinu,

melekh ha-olam,

asher kidshanu b'mitzvotav

v'tzivanu al biur ḥametz.

בָּרוּךְ אַתָּה, יְיָ אֱלֹהֵינוּ,

מֶלֶךְ הָעוֹלָם,

אֲשֶׁר קִדְּשָׁנוּ בְּמִצְוֹתָיו

וְצִוָּנוּ עַל בִּעוּר חָמֵץ.

Blessed are You, Adonai our God, Ruler of the world, who makes us holy with mitzvot and commands us to remove all the leaven from our home.

The candle holder leads the way and everyone else follows, peering into the darkness for stray crumbs of bread. Use the feather to scoop the crumbs into the wooden spoon or directly into the paper bag. When you have found all the crumbs, put the feather and the spoon in the bag and set it aside until morning.

The next morning burn the bag and its contents. You can light a small fire in the backyard or in your driveway. While the *ḥametz* burns, formalize its removal with the following words:

> *Any leaven that may still be in this house, which I have not seen or have not removed, shall be as if it does not exist and as the dust of the earth.*

From this moment the house is *pesaḥdik*—free of leaven. You are ready to celebrate the Passover holiday.

SECULAR DATES OF JEWISH HOLIDAYS

	1998	1999	2000	2001	2002	2003	2004	2005	2006	2007
Rosh Hashanah	Sept. 21	Sept. 11	Sept. 30	Sept. 18	Sept. 7	Sept. 27	Sept. 16	Oct. 4	Sept. 23	Sept. 13
Yom Kippur	Sept. 30	Sept. 20	Oct. 9	Sept. 27	Sept. 16	Oct. 6	Sept. 25	Oct. 13	Oct. 2	Sept. 22
Sukkot	Oct. 5	Sept. 25	Oct. 14	Oct. 2	Sept. 21	Oct. 11	Sept. 30	Oct. 18	Oct. 7	Sept. 27
Simḥat Torah	Oct. 13	Oct. 3	Oct. 22	Oct. 10	Sept. 29	Oct. 19	Oct. 8	Oct. 26	Oct. 15	Oct. 5
Hanukkah	Dec. 14	Dec. 4	Dec. 22	Dec. 10	Nov. 30	Dec. 20	Dec. 8	Dec. 26	Dec. 16	Dec. 5

	1999	2000	2001	2002	2003	2004	2005	2006	2007	2008
Tu B'Shevat	Feb. 1	Jan. 22	Feb. 8	Jan. 25	Jan. 18	Feb. 7	Jan. 25	Feb. 13	Feb. 3	Jan. 22
Purim	Mar. 2	Mar. 21	Mar. 9	Feb. 7	Mar. 18	Mar. 7	Mar. 25	Mar. 14	Mar. 4	Mar. 21
Passover	Apr. 1	Apr. 20	Apr. 8	Mar. 18	Apr. 17	Apr. 6	Apr. 24	Apr. 13	Apr. 3	Apr. 20
Yom Hashoah	Apr. 13	May 2	Apr. 20	May 6	Apr. 29	Apr. 18	May 6	Apr. 25	Apr. 15	May 2
Yom Ha–Atzma'ut	Apr. 21	May 10	Apr. 28	Apr. 17	May 7	Apr. 26	May 14	May 3	Apr. 23	May 10
Shavuot	May 21	June 9	May 28	May 6	June 6	May 26	June 13	June 2	May 23	June 9

The Rhythm of the Kitchen

"Make them days of

feasting and gladness…"

―――

MEGILLAT ESTHER 9:22

A Note on Kashrut

Any discussion of Jewish food would be incomplete without a few words on the tradition of "keeping kosher." The *mitzvah* of *sh'mirat kashrut*, observing the dietary laws, may seem complicated, but it can be broken into three basic parts: separation of meat and milk; prohibition of certain meats; and ritual slaughter of those meats that are allowed.

Within the tradition of the dietary laws, foods are grouped as either meat, dairy or *pareve* (neither meat nor dairy). Meat and dairy foods are kept separate. They are not cooked together or served or eaten together, and usually some period of time is allowed to elapse between meat and dairy meals. Separate sets of cooking and eating utensils are set aside for each. *Pareve* foods, on the other hand, may be cooked and eaten with either meat or dairy foods. Anything that grows in the ground is considered *pareve*, including fruits, vegetables, grains, and nuts. In addition, fish and eggs are considered *pareve*.

"You shall not boil a kid in its mother's milk."

EXODUS 34:26 AND DEUTERONOMY 14:21

Meats that are considered acceptable within the tradition of *kashrut* include most domesticated poultry, cattle, deer, sheep, and goats. Meat from mammals that do not have split hooves or do not chew their cud, such as pigs and rabbits, are considered unacceptable, or *trafe*. In addition, certain fish species (primarily those without scales and gills) are also deemed *trafe*, including crustaceans, shellfish, shark, and eels. Also, certain cuts of permitted animals are not kosher. Jews who keep kosher avoid these foods.

For those meats that are allowed, special handling is required under the strict application of the dietary laws. This includes ritual slaughter and the salting and soaking of meat to be sure no blood remains. Jews who are strict in their observance of *kashrut* generally obtain their meat from a kosher butcher, where operations are under the supervision of a rabbi.

In today's complex world of commercially produced foods from around the globe, seemingly simple foods such as bread, crackers, and breakfast cereals might be considered *pareve*, dairy, meat, or even *trafe*, depending on the ingredients used in producing them. For this reason, a series of symbols have been developed to help identify foods that adhere to the precepts of *kashrut*. These labels, including **K** and **U** are useful guides to searching out the many packaged foods that are acceptable within the tradition of *kashrut*.

Finally, you may notice at Passover that many foods appear with the label "Kosher for Passover." Because bread and other leavened foods are avoided during this time, special care is taken to assure consumers that none of these ingredients has been included in foods designed for the Passover table.

Recipes for the Holidays

Each holiday has its own special flavor. Holiday foods do more than satisfy our taste buds—they keep alive that old-time festival atmosphere that has always been a part of the Jewish experience. In this respect, we are just like every generation before us. We cannot imagine a happy celebration without delicious holiday foods. On the following pages you will find recipes for a few traditional favorites to get you started. They are easy to follow and they taste good, but most important, they can be prepared by parents and children together.

For Shabbat: Ḥallah

The Hebrew word *Ḥallah* actually refers not to the special Shabbat loaf itself, but to the ancient command to set aside a portion of bread for the priests of the Temple. After the destruction of the Temple, it became customary to take a small part of the dough and throw it into the fire, to represent this portion. Today the phrase "Ḥallah is taken" on packages of kosher bread and matzah tells us that this *mitzvah* has already been completed for us.

This is a two-part recipe; the dough must be refrigerated overnight.

1 package dry yeast	3 eggs
1/4 cup plus 2 tablespoons sugar	1/3 cup oil
1 cup lukewarm water	1/2 cup warm water
5 cups flour	1 1/4 to 1 1/2 cups flour
1 tablespoon plus 1 teaspoon salt	1 egg

On Thursday:

Add yeast and sugar to 1 cup of lukewarm water and stir until dissolved.

Put 5 cups of flour into a large bowl and make a well in the middle. Add salt, 3 eggs, oil, and yeast mixture and mix thoroughly.

Add 1/2 cup of warm water. Stir in additional 1 1/4 to 1 1/2 cups of flour to make a stiff yet easy-to-handle dough.

Turn the dough out on a floured surface and knead for several minutes until smooth, sprinkling with more flour if dough is sticky. Grease a large glass bowl and place the dough in the bowl, turning once so both sides are greased.

Cover with a towel and let the dough rise in a warm place for 1 hour. Dough will rise only slightly. Punch down the dough, cover it with plastic wrap and a towel, and refrigerate overnight.

On Friday:

Punch down the dough and make two loaves by dividing the dough into six pieces: Shape into strips and then braid, using three strips for each loaf. Pinch ends of strips together. Place on greased baking sheets.

Cover and let rise for 30 to 40 minutes in a warm place. Brush loaves lightly with a beaten egg. Bake at 350° for 30 to 35 minutes until golden brown. To test for doneness, a thump on the bottom should give a hollow sound.

For Rosh Hashanah: Taiglach

Honey for a sweet new year. Choose a bright, sunny day to make this honey candy. Moisture in the air will keep it from hardening.

2 eggs	1 cup honey
2 tablespoons vegetable oil	1/2 cup sugar
1 1/2 cups flour	1/2 teaspoon ground ginger
1/2 teaspoon salt	1 cup nuts, coarsely broken
3/4 teaspoon baking powder	

Beat eggs slightly. Add the oil and mix.

Sift the flour, salt, and baking powder together. Stir into the egg and oil mixture to make a soft but not sticky dough. Add more flour if necessary.

Place the dough on a board, lightly sprinkle with flour, and twist it into a rope shape about 1/3 inch thick. Dip a knife in flour, and cut the rope of dough into small pieces about 1/3 inch long.

Place the pieces on a well-greased shallow pan and bake in a moderately hot oven (375°) for about 10 minutes, or until slightly browned. Shake the pan a few times to keep the pieces separated and evenly browned.

Now prepare the honey syrup. Put the honey, sugar, and ginger in a saucepan and stir until the sugar is completely melted. Now cook it gently over a low flame for 5 minutes, stirring constantly, for honey will burn quickly.

Add the baked pieces of dough and the nuts. Stir gently over low heat until the mixture is a deep golden brown.

Pour out on a large platter or board wet with cold water.

Shape the candy into a cake about 8 inches square and 2 inches deep, using a knife wet with cold water. Cut into 2-inch strips and cut again into bite-sized pieces.

When cool, wrap in waxed paper.

Makes 36 to 48 pieces of candy.

For Sukkot: Apple Strudel

When the weather permits, we take our meals out in the *sukkah* and linger over a dessert bursting with the season's new fruit, enjoying these last beautiful days of fall.

For the dough	For the filling
2 1/2 cups flour	jam or marmalade
1/2 teaspoon baking powder	8 apples, pared and chopped
1/2 teaspoon salt	1 cup raisins, chopped
1/4 cup sugar	1 cup nuts, coarsely chopped
1 egg	sugar
1/2 cup oil	cinnamon
1/2 cup lukewarm water	oil, for brushing dough

Sift flour, baking powder, salt, and sugar into a mixing bowl. With a fork, beat together the egg, oil, and water. Make a well in the center of the flour mixture and into it drop the egg mixture. Then stir together to make a soft dough, one that is not sticky and is easy to handle.

Sprinkle a board lightly with flour. Divide the dough into three parts. Roll one piece of dough until it is paper thin. If it tears, mend it by pressing a piece of dough from the edge to the torn part. Spread the dough with a thin layer of jam or marmalade. Now sprinkle on 1/3 of the chopped apples, raisins, nuts, sugar, and cinnamon.

Roll the dough lengthwise like a jelly roll. Press the edges together to keep the filling in. Repeat these steps with the other two pieces of dough.

Place the three rolls on a well-greased baking sheet. Leave space between the rolls to allow them to bake evenly. Brush the top of each roll with oil, and sprinkle them with sugar and cinnamon.

Bake in a moderately hot oven (375°) for 45 minutes, or until golden brown. Remove from oven. When cool, cut into 1 1/2 inch slices.

Makes about 60 small pieces of strudel.

For Ḥanukkah: Latkes

Ḥanukkah means dedication. We celebrate freedom and the rededication of the Temple by eating foods that remind us of the oil that lasted eight days, allowing the Temple's *menorah* to burn without cease.

> 4 large potatoes
>
> 2 eggs
>
> 1 teaspoon salt
>
> 3 tablespoons flour
>
> 1/2 teaspoon baking powder
>
> oil for frying

Wash and peel potatoes. Grate by hand or with a food processor. Drain off most of the liquid. Beat eggs and mix all ingredients together, except oil.

Drop mixture by tablespoons into hot oil in skillet. Fry on both sides until brown, then drain on paper towels. Serve with applesauce or sour cream.

Serves 4

Note: Do not fry more than three or four latkes at the same time. Too many fried at once will cool the oil and keep the latkes from being crisp and tender.

For Tu B'Shevat: Schnecken

Although winter is still upon us, we know spring will be coming soon. We celebrate the earth, the trees, and the bounty they produce by sampling fruits and nuts of many kinds. These fruits and nut morsels make a tasty beginning.

1 envelope dried yeast	1 teaspoon vanilla
1/4 cup lukewarm water	4 1/2 cups all-purpose flour
1 teaspoon sugar	melted butter, for brushing dough
1/2 cup hot milk	sugar
1 teaspoon salt	cinnamon
3/4 cup sugar	raisins
2 eggs, well beaten	walnuts, coarsely broken
1 cup butter or vegetable fat, melted	

Stir the yeast into the lukewarm water. Stir the teaspoon of sugar into the yeast mixture, and set aside.

In a deep mixing bowl, stir the hot milk, salt, 3/4 cup sugar, and the 1 cup of melted butter or fat until the sugar is dissolved. Let the mixture cool to lukewarm. Then add the yeast and the eggs. Add the vanilla. Beat well together.

Add the flour, about a cup at a time, and beat it in well. Continue until all the flour is used and you have a ball of tender dough. Brush the dough with oil to keep it from drying while it rises. Cover with a clean towel and set in a warm, not hot, place until it doubles in bulk (about 2 hours).

Divide the dough into three parts. Roll out each piece on a lightly floured board. Roll the dough until it is 1/3 inch thick. Brush with melted butter. Sprinkle with sugar, cinnamon, raisins, and walnuts. Roll like a jelly roll and pinch the edges to keep the filling in. Cut the roll into 1-inch slices. Place the slices cut side down, about 1 inch apart, on a greased pie pan or other shallow baking pan.

Roll out the remaining two pieces of dough 1/3 inch thick and repeat as above. Cover the slices of schnecken with a clean towel and set to rise in a warm, not hot, place to double in bulk (about 2 hours). Brush again with melted butter. Bake in a moderately hot oven (375°F.) for 12 to 15 minutes or until nicely browned.

Makes about 48 schnecken.

For Purim: Hamantashen

What better way to get the better of Haman than by eating his hat! These three-cornered cookies are a delicious way to make Haman disappear.

> 1/2 cup butter or margarine
>
> 1 cup sugar
>
> 1 egg
>
> 1 tablespoon milk
>
> 1 teaspoon vanilla extract
>
> 2 cups flour
>
> 2 teaspoons baking powder
>
> 1/4 teaspoon salt
>
> fruit preserves, prune jam
> *(lekvar)* or poppy seeds *(mohn)*

Cream the butter and gradually add sugar. Beat the mixture until fluffy. Add egg, milk, and vanilla and beat well. Sift flour, baking powder, and salt together and add to mixture. Stir to make a soft dough. Chill in the refrigerator for 20 minutes.

Sprinkle a board lightly with flour. Roll the dough out on the board until it is about 1/8 inch thick. Dip a wide-mouthed jar or glass into flour and cut circles from the dough. Spoon some preserves or jam in the center of each circle and bring three sides of the circle together to form a triangle, leaving about one-third open in the center. Pinch the edges together to make a seam.

Arrange well apart on an ungreased baking sheet. Bake in a hot oven (400°) for 10 to 12 minutes.

Makes about 36 hamantashen.

For Passover: Matzah Balls

Matzoh balls are the traditional replacement for noodles in chicken soup during Passover. Some cooks hide an almond in the center of each as a special crunchy surprise.

    2 eggs

    1/4 cup water

    3 tablespoons melted shortening

    1 teaspoon salt

    dash of pepper

    1/2 cup matzah meal

Beat the eggs lightly with a fork. Add the water, melted shortening, salt, and pepper, and mix well. Add the matzah meal and stir thoroughly. Refrigerate for 1 hour.

Wet your hands and form the mixture into small balls. Drop balls into a large pot of boiling water or chicken soup. Cover and simmer 20 to 25 minutes. Serve in chicken soup.

Makes about 16 matzah balls.

For Yom Ha-Azma'ut: Falafel

What better way to rejoice in Israel's independence than by sampling these savory morsels: modern Israel's ubiquitous street food.

> 2 cups chickpeas, soaked in water overnight
>
> 1 medium onion, chopped
>
> 1 clove garlic, minced
>
> 2 tablespoons parsley, finely chopped
>
> 1 egg, lightly beaten
>
> 1–2 teaspoons ground cumin
>
> 1 teaspoon ground coriander
>
> 1/2 teaspoon baking soda
>
> 1/2 teaspoon salt
>
> dash Tabasco
>
> 1/2 cup bulghar wheat, soaked in water for one hour
>
> vegetable oil for frying

Drain chickpeas and mash well in a food processor. Add onion and garlic; process briefly. Add parsley, egg, spices, baking soda, salt, and Tabasco. Process until well combined.

Drain bulghar wheat. Add to chickpeas and process until mixture forms a soft ball.

Refrigerate for one hour or more.

With two teaspoons, or a falafel maker, form mixture into small balls about 1 1/2 inches in diameter. Heat deep fryer or heavy pot filled with oil to a depth of 2–3 inches. Fry falafel balls 3 or 4 at a time until golden brown. Drain on paper towels.

Serve immediately on pita bread with hummus, tahine, chopped cucumber, tomatoes, and lettuce.

Makes about 24 falafel.

For Shavuot: Cheese Blintzes

As the saying goes, the Torah is as nourishing as milk and honey. We savour sweet, rich blintzes and celebrate the joy we feel that the Torah is ours.

For the pancake

>   2 eggs
>
>   1/2 teaspoon salt
>
>   1 cup milk
>
>   1 cup flour, sifted
>
>   butter

For the filling

>   1 pound dry cottage cheese
>   or farmer cheese
>
>   1 egg
>
>   salt and pepper or sugar
>   to taste

Beat 2 eggs with salt until light and fluffy. Stir in milk and add to sifted flour to make a smooth, thin batter.

Melt a very small amount of butter in a 6-inch skillet.

Pour in just enough batter to cover bottom of pan (about 2 tablespoons) and tilt the pan from side to side. Cook gently for a minute or two until edges of blintz dry and pull away from pan.

Turn out with sharp tap onto a towel to cool.

Stack them after they cool.

Blend cottage cheese, egg, and salt and pepper or sugar in blender or with electric mixer until smooth.

Place a heaping tablespoon of filling on the fried side of each pancake. Fold three sides over the cheese filling. Then roll the pancake, tucking in the edges to keep the filling in.

Fry in butter or oil until golden brown, turning once. Or bake in 350° oven until crisp and brown.

Serve with sour cream or jam.

Makes 16 blintzes.